Marcelo Baena Moreno

Creating a Winning Business CV

Through hundreds of outstanding professional
accomplishments in the 21 main business domains

- Target-audience: students, undergraduates and graduates in any area of knowledge but that work in the business arena

- Persuasive and successful communication for the crucial task of enchanting current and potential employers

1st Edition in English, Charleston, 2016

A correct manner to cite this piece of work is:

Moreno, M. B. (2016) Creating a Winning Business CV – Through hundreds of outstanding professional accomplishments in the 21 main business domains, 1st Edition in English, Marcelo Baena Moreno, Charleston, United States, 171 pages

Disclaimer

The author strived to publish reliable data and information, but the author cannot be responsible for either the validity of the information presented or the consequences that the reader faces by using them. The author consulted plagiarism detection computer software, and concluded that the information contained in this book practically doesn't present correlation with the analyzed database, which would seem to be one of the widest in the editorial market.

To my Family and my Friends

Contents

Preface

This first edition of 'Creating a Winning Business CV' was written to guide students and graduates about what professional accomplishments in business are possible, desirable and preferable to promote them to current and potential employers. The main advantage of the book is that it states directly the teachings, and invites the reader to adapt them to his or her own CV. Across the publication, the professional accomplishments are proposed in the 21 main business subjects: Corporate Governance, Strategy, Business Administration, Organizational Culture, Law, Operations Management, Negotiation, Marketing, Foreign Trade, Supply Management, Human Resources, Organizational Behavior, Accounting, Credit Management, Finance, Economics, Insurance, Quality Management, Environmental Management, Social Responsibility and Real Estate. **Well, to be the owner of a Winning Business CV, having one or more of these subjects is enough, and within them the majority of subtitles and the majority of professional accomplishments are expected, in case you wish to present a detailed CV, or a selection among these accomplishments, in case you intend to present a one-page CV.**

About the Author

Occupying important executive positions at outstanding companies both domestically and internationally, the author wrote this book while he was carrying out, in the last 20 years, a good deal of the professional accomplishments that the book presents. His academic background consists of the Civil Engineering course (Universidade Estadual de Campinas) and the Master in Air Transport and Airports (Instituto Tecnologico de Aeronautica), in Brazil.

Introduction

In the 3rd Millennium, people worldwide have wide and sometimes unrestricted access to information through the internet and at the same time higher education is reached more easily nowadays than it was reached some decades ago. Training workshops take place in companies in order to enable staff of several departments operate complex information systems. In this way, professionals are looking for some means to constantly hone their skills to carry out tasks that demand each time more decision-making at all hierarchical levels.

Within this context of greater freedom for professionals, opportunities arise to develop tasks with innovation potential and decisive contribution for the survival and growth of companies, which fight relentlessly to position their products and services as the most searched by the clientele.

However, these opportunities for contribution are not seized many times as they should because professionals lack a guide enumerating the possible, desirable and preferable accomplishments. Yet this book is intended to be this guide, bringing ideas of activities that make a difference and promote executives both to their current and to their potential employers, who are responsible for rewarding good practices, through positive feedback, providing quality of life at work, leisure/work balance and more attractive compensation packages.

This book presents hundreds of ideas for winning professional accomplishments, which make a professional stand out in the crowd as an example to be followed and that are decisive for the sought-after operational and strategic success of micro, small, medium and large companies. The starting point of these accomplishments is the book's references, hence consulting them is recommended.

The book is divided into five chapters. The brief **Chapter 1 – Personal Data** deals with the initial presentation and the contacting data of the CV's owner. Following, **Chapter 2 – Higher Education** aims at highlighting intellectual accomplishments carried out at teaching institutions or conducted outside them during the long period of university studies. Yet **Chapter 3 – Business Experience** is the main part of the book, in which the winning accomplishments of the business professional are presented and discussed. They are grouped in 21 main business subjects: Corporate Governance, Strategy, Business Administration, Organizational Culture, Law, Operations Management, Negotiation, Marketing, Foreign Trade, Supply Management, Human Resources, Organizational Behavior, Accounting, Credit Management, Finance, Economics, Insurance, Quality Management, Environmental Management, Social Responsibility and Real Estate. Subsequently, it comes **Chapter 4 – Information Technology Experience,** that tells the minimum level of knowledge in computing required for career advancement and the level required for those who want to stand out in this regards. Finally, but not less importantly, **Chapter 5 – International Experience** is reached, which organizes the mastery of foreign languages and the relationship with foreign countries.

Throughout the book, the capital letters of the alphabet 'X' and 'Y' appear several times. When they appear, they should be mentally substituted by a number, percentage, word or phrase that, according to the candidate's career, corresponds to a true statement about his or her academic and professional history.

In order to finish this introduction, it is opportune to acknowledge that the objective of this piece of work goes beyond bringing ready-to-use phrases to be transferred to your CV. Because people have varying individual characteristics, as well as own professional and academic backgrounds, new ideas adapted to the readers themselves will be generated, based on this data input. The book can also be used as textbook in 'Introduction to Business Administration' and 'Business Career Management' undergraduate courses.

Good Reading!

Chapter 1 – Personal Data

The minimum indispensable personal information in the CV is the full name and the data for preferred immediate contact, that is, either the e-mail address, or the residential phone number, or the mobile phone number, or even all the three.

The citation of the residential address enables the recruiter to know the proximity to the working place or to the consumer market (for the case of external sales' professionals). This information can help the person that recruits to calculate possible future monthly expenses with transportation. For vacancies located in other cities which demand a change of fixed residence, the candidate must mention that he or she is (or will be when the labor contract starts) apt and available for this new situation. In the case of a city located overseas, it can be useful for the selection process to inform the nationality, place and date of birth, or even a possible double citizenship (in case the candidate possesses).

It can be interesting and appropriate to mention a blog or internet website kept by the vacancy's aspirer in case there is a positive correlation between the subject treated in that virtual address and the field of the vacancy's advertiser or even that one skill demonstrated in that place is pertinent for the desired job position. Besides, an increasing number of recruiting professionals, be it implicitly or explicitly, search for information and come to conclusions about candidates' personal characteristics through their profiles in far-reaching social networks and number of followers. Hence, it is up to the candidate the decision of informing or not about his or her participation in these networks, as well as behaving properly inside them, in order not only not spoil a wonderful track of professional accomplishments, but also make them promote him or her in hiring decisions.

Finally, regarding framing, it is suggested to centralize the personal data at the top of the page. Should the candidate decide to include all the information discussed previously, it will fit approximately four lines. It is recommended that the full name be written in bold letters and that the last surname be written in capital letters. Moreover, the combination between font type and size should denote seriousness, for instance, Microsoft Times New Roman sizes 11 or 12, or even, Arial sizes 10 or 11. For the sake of consistency, the chosen combination should be used in the other sections of the CV. Hereunder follows the suggested positioning for the personal data:

Name Surname SURNAME

Street, number – City – Province – Country – ZIP code

Home: 0000-0000 – Mobile: 0000-0000 – Email

Nationality – Place and Date of Birth

Chapter 2 – Higher Education

Professional business life requires a minimum of university studies. This minimum varies according to the activities and responsibilities of each job position. Besides the business majors themselves (Business Administration, Law, Economics, Marketing, Accounting, and so on), many other majors can be useful for business job positions, in a case by case analysis (such as Engineering, Medicine, and many more). The presentation of majors should preferably start from the most recent and probably higher level achieved, that is, possibly graduate studies followed by undergraduate studies. The basic information is the major name and respective level, the name of the higher education institution, its location and beginning and ending years, that can be accompanied by either one or several outstanding academic and professional accomplishments, when pertinent, in a detailed CV, or the main accomplishment in a one-page CV, such as the suggestions below:

Beginning – End University, City, Country
> *Name of the graduate course*
> (Specialization, Master or Doctorate)

-       GPA = X% (Top Y% in class)
-       Score in the Exam X = Y% (the international examinations are GMAT, GRE General, GRE Subject, TOEIC, TOEFL and IELTS, but some countries do offer their own examinations, that is the reason why the candidate should check with his or her teaching institution). For details about the GMAT, access www.gmac.com, regarding GRE General Test and GRE Subject Test, visit www.ets.org/gre, further information on TOEIC is found at www.ets.org/toeic, about TOEFL visit www.ets.org/pt/toefl and regarding IELTS see www.ielts.org.
-       Internship carried out at 'Company', City, Country (12 weeks), having developed 'the following activities'
-       International Exchange at 'Institution', City, Country (3 months)
-       Final Research, Dissertation or Thesis named 'Title'
-       Presentation of the technical paper 'Title' at 'Conference' ('Year')
-       Publication of the technical article 'Title' at 'Journal' ('Year')

Beginning – End   University, City, Country

Name of the major

- Ranked X^{th} in the admission examination among Y applicants

- Ranked X^{th} in the admission examination among Y registered students

- Admitted for the first time in the second year of high school

- GPA = X% (Top Y% in class)

- Score in the exam X = Y% (The candidate must check which national examination of secondary level his or her university adopts in the selection process)

- Teacher's assistant receiving scholarship in the subject "Name" (1 year)

- Scientific Initiation Scholarship about "Subject" (1 year)

- Final Research named 'Title'

- Winner of the 'Award', organized by the 'Entity' ('Year')

- X^{th} finalist in the competition 'Subject', organized by 'Entity' ('Year')

- International Exchange at 'University', City, Country (1 year)

- Volunteer of the NGO 'Denomination' ('Period') developing 'the following activities' and attaining 'the following results'

- Technical Visit at 'Company', City, Country, where 'the following facilities' and 'the following production process' were shown to manufacture 'the final product' ('Year')

- Apprenticeship at 'Organization', City, Country, carrying out 'the following activities' and achieving 'the following results' ('Duration')

- Organizer of the 'Event', City, Country, for the 'target-audience' ('Year')

Chapter 3 – Business Experience

Business experience is sometimes preceded by an item called 'professional objective'. This insertion is up to the candidate, since it can be omitted if the professional history supplies clear indication of what this objective is and has been throughout the career. In case the vacancy means a change in the career direction, the Professional objective must be stated and justified.

The minimum professional information begins by basic data in bold letters such as company name, city, country, starting and ending month and year and job positions. In a case by case analysis, it can also be useful to illustrate complementary data such as business field, annual operational turnover, number of employees, internet website, compensation and time spent in each job position, as follows:

Beginning   **Company, City, Country**
End   **Field – Turnover – Employees – Website**
           Job 1 – Compensation (duration)
           Job... – Compensation ... (duration)
           Current Job – Compensation (duration)

The activities developed by the professional within the company begin thereafter. In this book, high level business activities are defined as those that fit one of the 21 proposed topics: Corporate Governance, Strategy, Business Administration, Organizational Culture, Law, Operations Management, Negotiation, Marketing, Foreign Trade, Supply Management, Human Resources, Organizational Behavior, Accounting, Credit Management, Finance, Economics, Insurance, Quality Management, Environmental Management, Social Responsibility and Real Estate. Candidates are not expected to possess professional accomplishments in all of the presented topics, let alone copy and paste this information literally to their own CVs. In order to be the owner of a Winning Business CV, having one or more of these subjects is enough, and within them the majority of subtitles and the majority of professional accomplishments are expected, in case you wish to present a detailed CV, or a selection among these accomplishments, in case you intend to present a one-page CV. And the CV must not be general, but adapted to the desired vacancy, that is, highlighting the most important professional accomplishments for the aspired vacancy, always reflecting the candidate's character.

3.1.Corporate Governance

Corporate Governance constitutes a system that oversees the main executives' behavior and work in order to prevent their carrying out actions that end up benefiting only themselves in detriment of other stakeholders, from which the shareholders are most important ones. Following are the professional accomplishments regarding this subject:

CORPORATE GOVERNANCE:

Strategic Management: *Planning*: (1) Familiar with the Sarbanes-Oxley Act of 2002 [1]; (2) Designed a corporate governance system for the company, determining the number of directors, mandate length and number of meetings per year; (3) Developed corporate governance policies; (4) Defined how many and which other companies' Boards our CEO was allowed to participate in; (5) Organized elections for Board Members [2]; (6) Evaluated decision criteria to be used in elections and Chose the most appropriate for our case; *Execution*: (1) Dealt with the media regarding accounting scandals; (2) Gathered evidence to respond to lawsuits; (3) Kept agency costs lower than system implementation and running costs; (4) Detected where earnings have been massaged; (5) Appointed some independent directors; (6) Reviewed the effectiveness of internal controls [3]; (7) Gave shareholders greater influence over elections and executive compensation; (8) Had investors pay a X% premium for our well-governed company; (9) Contracted a director and officer liability insurance; (10) Increased by X% the total percentage of shareholder return yearly and (11) Monitored KPIs to determine management's success and award compensation

Committees: *Planning*: (1) Organized the board committees [4]; (2) Created specialized committees when required [5]; *Audit committee*: (1) Examined integrity of published financial statements [6]; (2) Worked with management to set the parameters for accounting quality; (3) Oversaw regulatory compliance within the company [7]; (4) Received and Handled complaints about the company's accounting; (5) Engaged employees and the nonfinancial regulator in fraud detection; (6) Created a checklist to monitor CEO behavior regarding the potential need of restatements resulting from fraud; (7) Changed the auditor every X years; (8) Oversaw the relationship between external auditor and our company [8]; (9) Established whistleblower hotlines [9]; (10) Monitored internal control processes [10]; *Compensation committee*: (1) Set CEO compensation package (salary, bonus, stock options and perquisites) and Tied it to long-term performance targets [11]; (2) Conceded to executives and directors equity participation; (3) Explained compensation philosophy; (4) Allowed shareholders a say-on-pay; (5) Attracted, Retained and Motivated the CEO; (6) Allowed for a severance package after retirement; *Governance committee*: (1) Evaluated and Improved the company's governance structure and processes [12]; *Nominating committee*: (1) Developed a CEO succession plan [13]; (2) Created a skills-and-experience profile [14]; (3)

Identified, Interviewed and Evaluated candidates [15]; (4) Bossed competitions for CEO positions; (5) Disclosed candidates' academic and professional background to shareholders; (6) Built consensus around a favorite candidate [16]; (7) Provided smooth transitions for internal candidates for CEO positions; (8) Terminated poor performing CEOs [17]; _Risk committee_: (1) Identified and Assessed risks [18]; (2) Managed financial, reputational and compliance risks [19]; (3) Disclosed risks to shareholders [20]; (4) Developed a risk management culture [21]; (5) Defined risk policies [22]; (6) Issued risk reports [23]; (7) Determined the organization's risk profile [24] and (8) Ensured the corporation is operating at an adequate risk level [25]

Executive equity ownership: (1) Established a parallel between the executive's equity and his/her actions [26]; (2) Issued a document and Collected the CEO's signature for the commitment to disclose information when available, not when preferable and (3) Prevented executives from engaging in short-term trading [27]

Mergers and Acquisitions: (1) Protected against hostile takeovers [28]; (2) Encouraged friendly acquisitions [29]; (3) Disapproved executives from carrying out acquisitions by imitation of colleagues acting in the market [30]; (4) In mergers, Chose the company to be announced as being bought [31]; (5) Awarded a package of benefits to our CEO when our company was taken over [32]; (6) Monitored the target company in order to forecast the use of antitakeover mechanisms [33]; (7) Understood the motives of potential acquirers [34] and (8) Eliminated antitakeover provisions that did not truly protected shareholder interests [35]

Institutional shareholders and activist investors: (1) Encouraged block-holders to exercise monitoring of managerial performance and compensation [36]; (2) Assisted institutional shareholders in hiring a highly reputed advisory firm [37]; (3) Assisted institutional shareholders in sensitive issues being voted and (4) Adjusted plans to be voted to gain approval of institutional shareholders

Ratings: (1) Compared metrics within our industry published by institutions that measure the effectiveness of governance systems [38]; (2) Had all directors participate in education programs accredited by institutions that measure the effectiveness of governance systems and (3) Issued a press release saying that the company improved its corporate governance ratings

3.2.Strategy

Strategy comprehends planning and execution of actions and decisions that aim to guide the overall activities of the company. The professional activities concerning this subject are presented hereunder:

STRATEGY:

Planning: _Organization_: (1) Determined our company's strengths and weaknesses [1]; (2) Developed an explicit strategy [2]; (3) Committed to the chosen strategy [3]; (4) Demonstrated fit to the environment we work at and to the resources we own [4]; (5) Planned capacity expansion in the long-run [5]; (6) Decided to operate in the global marketplace [6]; _Industry_: (1) Gathered data on the industries we belong to [7]; (2) Analyzed our industry [8]; (3) Decided in which new industries to operate [9]; (4) Identified entry and exit barriers in these industries [10]; _Competitors_: (1) Developed a competitor intelligence system [11]; (2) Collected information on competitors' likely and declared goals and values [12]; (3) Identified competitors' strategies, attitudes and skills [13]; (4) Analyzed our competitors; their shown and contractual commitments [14] and the relative importance of markets they play in; (5) Discovered how their executives are motivated and rewarded [15]; (6) Determined the competitors' actual positions in the market and whether they perceive that way [16] and (7) Built a checklist for evaluating the competitor's defensive ability [17]

Execution: *Prevention of competitors' entry*: (1) Decreased the marginal cost of produced items whilst Increased the production output [18]; (2) Added ancillary services to our offers [19]; (3) Created switching costs for customers [20]; (4) Took part in industries that required huge capital investments to be feasible [21]; (5) Developed loyal distribution channels that as a result were unwilling to accommodate new entrants [22]; *Level of industrial competition*: (1) Entered industries with low level of competition [23], those in which there is always room for growth upon the staff members' efforts; *Availability of substitute products*: (1) Identified substitutes [24]; (2) Included substitutes to our core products in our product line [25]; *Negotiation with Clients*: (1) Chose the least influential customers on our organization's selling prices [26]; (2) Provided technical assistance [27]; (3) Selected customers with the lowest costs of servicing [28]; (4) Found buyers whose needs our company is in the best relative position to serve [29]; (5) Sold to organizations that are less likely to shift to substitutes [30]; (6) Discovered and Advertised a solid advantage of our products against substitutes [31]; (7) Located our company near a market from where competitors are far away [32]; (8) Preferred to serve buyers whose penalty for product failure is high relative to its cost [33]; (9) Chose buyers whose high profitability enables them to pass on to their clientele the cost of inputs [34]; (10) Focused on clients that are less sensitive to price [35] variations when these generally occur; (11) Dealing with price-sensitive decision makers, Persuaded them to reduce this sensibility [36]; (12) Widened product functions [37]; _Negotiation with Suppliers_: (1) Participated at industries whose suppliers are less concentrated [38]; (2) Qualified a pool of substitutes for our suppliers, their products and our company's employees in the labor market [39]; (3) Carried out shares of our purchases with each competing sellers [40]; (4) Enhanced our company's negotiating power [41]; (5) Denied products that require customized service [42]; _Negotiation with Competitors_: (1) Planned series of consecutive moves for the event of a myriad of potentially likely situations [43]; (2) Determined the probability of a warfare in each case [44]; (3) Brainstormed multiple bargaining alternatives [45]; (4) Rewarded competitors for not attacking our business pillars [46]; (5) Enhanced our profitability and simultaneously Didn't compromise competitors' growth [47]; (6) Assessed the inherent risks that competitors may pose by behaving both expectedly and unexpectedly; (7) Estimated timing of responses from competitors [48]; (8) Influenced the competitors' replies in a manner that ultimately benefited our organization; (9) Understood reasons behind actions [49]; (10)

Created a situation in which the competitors face goal dilemmas [50]; (11) Fostered to our competitors the idea that their moves were unwise [51]; (12) Established a logical pricing policy [52]; (13) Revealed discretionarily information to the market [53]; (14) Signaled actions truthfully when convenient and untruthfully whenever there was a need to do so besides an apparent reason could be built around the signal and (15) Listed historical signals from competitors [54], corresponding notified reasons and true underlying reasons that our company came to know later on

3.3.Business Administration

Business Administration consists of employing financial resources, allocating materials and human capital, carrying out activities and satisfying organizational objectives. Below are presented the professional accomplishments in this regard:

BUSINESS ADMINISTRATION:

<u>Planning</u>: *Culture*: (1) Determined the values, people and culture that are adequate to achieve our goals [1]; (2) Told newcomers the founder's story, highlighting his hard working despite his modest origin; (3) Created a slogan for the company [2]; (4) Created an annual ceremony to award a golden plate to the best employees [3]; (5) Linked cultural values to business performance [4]; (6) Reinforced cultural vision through words and actions [5]; *Strategic*: (1) Developed short, medium and long-term strategic plans [6]; (2) Built optimistic, expected and pessimistic scenarios [7]; (3) Chose challenging but realistic goals [8]; (4) Set performance standards; (5) Set contingency plans for crisis, emergencies and unexpected events [9]; (6) Switched to renewable energy sources; (7) Determined adequate responses to an uncertain environment [10]; (8) Focused efforts on our most loyal clientele base; (9) Delivered superior customer value [11]; (10) Guessed the future right; (11) Fostered our vision to our business network [12]; (12) Involved employees in strategic thinking and execution [13]; *Operational*: (1) Translated strategic plans into activities scheduled to meet objectives [14]; (2) Exercised time management [15]; (3) Allocated resources, schedules and tasks; (4) Split strategic goals into departmental tactical goals [16]; (5) Managed operational factors required to achieve objectives [17]; (6) Selected specific quantitative

measures to check whether goals are being met [18]; (7) Defined time horizons for activities [19]; _Ethics_: (1) Was appointed Chief Ethics Officer [20]; (2) Created an ethics' committee [21]; (3) Defined a corporate code of ethics [22]; (4) Discussed ethical dilemmas with employees as soon as they arose [23] and Forwarded the conclusions on them through internal newsletters; (5) Mapped stakeholders regarding expectations, needs, importance and relative power; (6) Created a training seminar on ethics; (7) Disciplined wrongdoers [24]; (8) Created a toll-free confidential ethics hotline [25] and (9) Evaluated the outcome of ethical efforts [26]

Organizing: _General_: (1) Updated the company profile to send to clients and suppliers; _Structure_: (1) Designed the vertical [27] and horizontal [28] structure of the organization; (2) Fulfilled the organization chart [29]; (3) Matched leadership styles and beliefs with the proposed structure [30]; (4) Defined clear lines of authority and formal reporting relationships [31]; (5) Ensured proper coordination of staff within and between departments [32]; (6) Created new names for existing and new positions; _Human Resources_: (1) Analyzed current HR department strategy and proposed modifications to it; (2) Right-sized the organization [33]; (3) Determined future staffing requirements [34]; (4) Trained the Chief HR Officer; (5) Defined acceptable professional dressing standards; (6) Retained the right people after a merger, acquisition or downsizing [35]; (7) Branded the company as an employer of choice [36]; _Employee motivation_: (1) Designed jobs to improve motivation [37]; (2) Empowered employees to carry out assignments [38]; (3) Engaged employees in goal setting and decision making processes [39]; (4) Focused on intrinsic rewards but also Applied extrinsic ones [40]; (5) Thanked staff; (6) Reduced inequity [41]; (7) Helped staff meet higher levels of needs [42]; (8) Appraised performance [43]; (9) Rewarded employees based on company performance [44]

Leading: _Communication_: (1) Fostered an open communication climate [45]; (2) Performed networking [46]; (3) As a speaker, Created clear messages and Selected appropriate communication channels [47]; (4) As a listener, Deciphered the meaning of messages and Offered feedback [48]; (5) Built critical reasoning skills; (6) Paraphrased what was said [49]; (7) Weighted the evidence [50]; (8) Conducted win-win conversations [51]; _Teams_: (1) Developed an effective team of subordinates [52]; (2) Set group norms [53]; (3) Created compelling team purposes [54]; (4) Shaped team culture [55]; (5) Monitored progress [56]; (6) Rewarded members [57]; (7) Defined team size and member roles [58]; (8) Initiated ideas [59]; (9) Managed team conflicts [60]; (10) Balanced conflict and cooperation [61]; _Global Environment_: (1) Sent top management to far away target countries to gather information on the customer market there [62]; (2) Developed a global mindset [63]; (3) Expanded our off-shoring activities [64]; (4) Sought cheaper labor and materials overseas [65]; (5) Designed products with worldwide appeal [66]; (6) Learned and Abided by international rules and regulations [67]; _Innovation_: (1) Launched a competition for new feasible innovative ideas [68]; (2) Presented an idea to solve a difficult but recurring problem [69]; (3) Introduced a practice that enhanced customer satisfaction; (4) Brought about organizational change [70]; (5) Was responsible for a major operational improvement that saved X thousand dollars; (6) Implemented a technology change [71]; (7) Motivated the R&D department to bring about more innovative products; (8) Developed a selection test to measure the creative potential of candidates; (9) Accepted mistakes and Rewarded risk-taking in the pursuit of cost savings; (10) Gathered the viewpoint of customers and suppliers when developing products; *Project Management*: (1) Carried out the opening of X branch offices in Y cities, including the development of a schedule for implementing public utilities, furniture and hiring staff; (2) Created a party at Head Office to celebrate sales records, what involved bringing a buffet and serving food; *Fleet Management*: (1) Planned purchasing, sales and maintenance of the company's car fleet

Controlling: _General_: (1) Created key performance indicators for all fields of the Balanced Scorecard [72]; (2) Fed the Balanced Scored Card with facts & figures [73]; (3) Controlled the Balanced Scorecard [74]; (4) Defined expense and revenue budgets [75]; (5) Analyzed financial statements and P&L statements [76]; (6) Decentralized the control of the company [77]; (7) Monitored both quantitative and qualitative performance; (8) Carried out a benchmarking analysis [78]; (9) Either Provided reinforcement or Took corrective action [79]; (10) Provided feedback on executive performance; (11) Produced information to take actions about Planning, Organizing and Leading; (12) Changed plans to meet shifting conditions [80]; (13) Continually Evaluated the competitive position of the company; (14) Calculated the annual business growth rate; _Decision-making_: (1) Planned programmed decisions for recurring problems [81]; (2) Considered what-if scenarios for non-programmed decisions [82]; (3) Acquired a company; (4) Built a new factory; (5) Developed a new product or service; (6) Entered a new geographical market; (7) Relocated headquarters to another city; (8) Formulated problems and Solved them [83]; (9) Gathered information [84]; (10) Defined criteria to evaluate alternative courses of action [85]; (11) Agreed on problem priorities [86]; (12) Analyzed possible root causes of problems [87]; (13) Developed alternatives [88]; (14) Selected and Implemented chosen alternatives [89]; (15) Evaluated and Provided feedback on presented solutions [90]; _Organizational Behavior_: (1) Based on chosen career values [91], Developed high-performance work attitudes [92]; (2) Evaluated the suitability of problem-solving styles and Chose one [93]; (3) Fostered the need for corporate citizenship; (4) Organized screened information into patterns for interpretation and response; (5) Developed own emotional intelligence and that of chief executives [94]; (6) Performed a weekly review; (7) Sought and Mitigated root causes of stress [95] and (8) Provided wellness programs [96]

3.4. Organizational Culture

Organizational culture corresponds to the national, regional or professional aspects that guide the employees' behavior and beliefs. In the lines that follow, the professional accomplishments regarding this field of the business world are presented:

ORGANIZATIONAL CULTURE:

Strategic Management: *Macro-Cultures*: (1) Immersed foreign new hires in the company's culture; *Subcultures*: (1) Corrected behavior determined by subcultures when required and *Micro-cultures*: (1) Aligned professionals to form micro-cultures

Cultural Assumptions: *General*: (1) Reduced anxiety arising from problems related to assumptions [1]; (2) Formed desired cultural assumptions among new comers [2]; *Environmental adaptation*: (1) Chose the key performance indicator to pay primary attention [3]; (2) Classified tasks by priority; (3) Eliminated ambiguity; (4) Aligned the mission and goals with priorities [4] and key performance indicators; (5) Developed remedial strategies for mistakes [5]; *Company-wide integration*: (1) Established group boundaries and methods for inclusion and exclusion [6]; (2) Listed what we look for in a new staff member [7]; (3) Set norms of trust [8]; (4) Defined policies for providing rewards and punishments [9]; (5) In case of failures; Fostered the idea of evaluating why instead of who failed [10]; (6) Wrote stories to tell to newcomers [11]; *Facts & Opinions*: (1) Determined that strategic decisions be carried out by directors whilst operational ones by other employees; (2) Confronted a myriad of data sources to form opinions based on facts; *Time*: (1) Established a primary time orientation [12] for the company; (2) Selected the occasions to pay attention for other time horizons; (3) Set units of time to carry out activities [13]; (4) Gave our own definition for the terms related to time [14]; *Space*: (1) Adopted, without any modification, the country's cultural norms for distance in the various communications' situations; (2) Determined the most appropriate office layout [15]; *Religion & Politics*: (1) Preserved the company as a laic place; (2) Forbid employees to engage in political discussions at work; *Relationships*: (1) Motivated individualism or collectivism according to the situation [16]; (2) Decided which individual interests would be sacrificed and which would be protected [17]; (3) Opted out for a professional degree of emotionality [18] and (4) Searched for the reasons for success and failure of activities

Culture Creation: *Original Groups*: (1) Exemplified how the organizational culture must be [19]; *New Groups*: (1) Shaped and Reinforced the desired culture [20]; (2) Incorporated into our culture constructive ideas from employees [21]; (3) Improved own behavioral consistency [22]; (4) Possessed own numbers to discuss and present [23]; (5) Reacted to critical incidents and organizational crisis [24] and (6) Explained to candidates the criteria for recruitment and selection [25]

Culture Assessment: (1) Compared assessment methods [26]; (2) Selected the most appropriate ones; (3) Evaluated our organization's culture [27]; (4) Designed cultural surveys [28]; (5) Determined whether specific cultural aspects are related to the ongoing company's performance [29]; (6) Compared the assessment outcome with the desired organization's cultural profile [30]; (7) Compared organizations on selected cultural dimensions in order to carry out mergers, acquisitions and joint ventures [31]; (8) Tested about the presence or absence of problematic subcultures [32]; (9) Evaluated the degree of hierarchy [33] and (10) Determined the type of corporate governance orientation [34]

Culture Change: (1) Identified cultural strengths [35]; (2) Looked for what required change [36]; (3) Decided when to change practices but not culture; (4) Adapted cultural weaknesses to the environment; (5) Created something lasting; (6) Solved important problems; (7) Fostered creativity and innovation; (8) Planned careers; (9) Found out what was missing or inhibiting change [37]; (10) Solved succession problems [38]; (11) Improved the organization self-image; (12) Dealt with the media about scandals [39]; (13) Defined the change objectives concretely [40]; (14) Bossed a merger and Managed the cultural clash [41]; (15) Launched a culture change [42]; (16) Destroyed undesired cultural aspects [43]; (17) Led a disconfirmation process [44]; (18) Reduced employees' learning anxiety [45]; (19) Gathered a myriad of learning tools to bring about change [46]; (20) Taught new ways of thinking and behaving [47] and (21) Confirmed and Reinforced changes [48]

Leadership: *Learning organization*: (1) Identified learning potential and experience in applicants for vacancies; (2) Selected pro-active candidates [49]; (3) Committed the staff to the learning to learn [50]; (4) Generated new responses [51]; (5) Provided resources to learn [52]; (6) Committed the staff to open communication about tasks [53]; *Learning Leader*: (1) Articulated the vision [54]; (2) Changed the vision when it was required [55]; (3) Understood the company evolution [56]; (4) Gathered information from multiple sources [57]; (5) Kept up-to-date with news directly affecting our business; (6) Sought information on the culture of countries our company deals with [58]; (7) Understood the main aspects of the micro-cultures operating organization-wide [59]; (8) Detected cultural, sub-cultural and micro-cultural incompatibilities [60]; (9) In external partnerships, Identified the cause of cultural differences [61]; (10) Spent X months abroad to compare cultures [62]; *Culture Islands*: (1) Managed multi-cultural groups from the nationality and professional standpoints [63]; (2) Created some common ground [64] through online training; (3) Focused on cultural capacities and learning skills [65]; (4) Reflected on own assumptions [66]; (5) Considered other people's assumptions [67]; (6) Decided what to do in case a leader makes a mistake [68]; (7) Decided how to trust a colleague [69] and (8) Mastered the art of carrying out phone and internet dialogues with coworkers that are unlikely to be met in person [70]

3.5.Law

Hereunder follow the Professional accomplishments concerning the subject Law, which comprise planning and execution aspects of activities with legal implication:

LAW:

Planning: (1) Familiar with legal terms and (2) Planned the company's obedience to the national laws

Tax Law: *Strategy*: (1) Monitored tax-generating facts and respective rates [1]; (2) Analyzed which federal, state and municipal taxes the company must pay, which taxes the company receives credit for paying and those that the company is free from paying [2]; (3) Analyzed deadlines for paying taxes [3]; (4) Decided between framing the company's profit ascertainment as either actual or presumed; *Declarations*: (1) Gathered information from the company's owners, Fulfilled and Submitted tax statements; (2) Got permission to operate in a free trade zone; *Crime prevention*: (1) Classified merchandise in the correct, exact and habitual manners in the markets where the company operates; (2) Assured the invoice issuance for all operations with merchandises (entry and exit) and the corresponding availability of digital files to the accountant; (3) Selected accountants by indication; (4) Forwarded the questions made by the state revenue official to our accountant, who demonstrated the soundness of our business; (5) Supplied to our accountant bank statements at the end of each fiscal year; (6) Assured that taxes were paid within deadlines [4] and (7) Supplied to the accountant invoices of the products we purchased in the domestic market

Labor Law: *Sources*: (1) With the aid of the syndicate representative and employees, Updated entirely the collective agreement [5]; (2) Wrote up the company's regulations [6]; (3) Revised clauses of new labor contracts in order to benefit the employer; *Disciplinary Power*: (1) Applied penalties to wrongdoers [7]; *Types of Employees*: (1) Regarding apprentices and temporary labor workers [8], Analyzed if our company would hire them ; *Remuneration*: (1) Paid all the employees monthly [9]; (2) Practiced salary isonomy [10]; (3) Discussed possible compensation values during selection interviews; (4) Set 44 working hours a week [11]; (5) Stipulated salaries above the minimum legal wage; (6) Behaved smoothly toward employees that had few non-justified absences (or unwarranted justified absences); (7) Established participation of the employees in the company's profits and outcomes [12]; *Vacation*: (1) Opted out for non-collective vacation periods [13]; *Redundancy*: (1) Gathered evidence of acts practiced by employees that would allow well-grounded redundancy [14]; *Strikes* [15]: (1) Made some possible concessions during a strike so that is would finish; (2) Negotiated continually with the syndicate; *Safety*: (1) Created an Internal Commission for Accident Prevention [16]; *Processes*: (1) Gathered evidence; (2) Replied irregularities' complaints; (3) Assisted in the writing up of processes; (4) Participated in audiences as a witness; (5)

Followed up processes from the pledge or citation until the verdict; _Crime Prevention_: (1) Denied forced and compulsory labor [17]; (2) Denied child labor [18] and (3) Accepted the freedom of association and the collective negotiation [19]

Civil Law: *Processes*: (1) Advised the organization's lawyer on inclusions and exclusions of sentences in a process of property litigation; (2) Assisted in the writing up of a process for the reimbursement of paid values to an external professional for malpractice; (3) In a process of importation costs' reimbursement of a defaulting client, Gathered documents [20] and Analyzed to our benefit the equity contract's clauses of one of our offshore companies; *Assets*: (1) Managed the company's assets and those private of the company's owners; *Real Estate*: (1) With the purchasing contract of an acquired building, Requested its notarized registration; (1) Asked for the city official a certificate stating that the city is the only confronting party (public streets) to our building that occupies the entire block; (2) Demanded to the notary the surface rectification; (3) Demanded to the notary the unification of pieces of land; (4) Calculated the total delayed rent value to sue a tenant for payment default; *Authorship*: (1) Reformulated the clauses of a software use license agreement to make it evident the intellectual right [21] of the company's owner as the author of the computer program flowchart; *Succession*: (1) Participated at a course on Family Holding Companies; (2) Advised the owners not to make a Family Holding Company

Commercial Law: *Societies*: (1) Submitted modifications to the company's equity contract; *Banks*: (1) Fulfilled forms and Gathered documents to open an overseas bank account; *New businesses*: (1) Wrote up a letter of intention to develop a building in order to receive the donation of a piece of land from the city; *Intellectual Property*: (1) Created and Renewed brands and patents [22]; *Bankruptcies*: Due to the high debt volume, Pleaded the client's bankruptcy

3.6. Operations Management

In the lines that follow, the professional accomplishments in terms of Operations Management are listed, corresponding to manufacturing products and making services available:

OPERATIONS MANAGEMENT:

Strategy: (1) Created operational policies; (2) Evaluated costs [1] and (3) Set prices [2]

Forecasting: (1) Decided what to forecast [3]; (2) Chose a forecasting method [4]; (3) Selected an accuracy level [5]; (4) Carried out forecasts [6]; (5) Determined trends [7] and (6) Evaluated unforeseen events

Building: *Capacity*: (1) Determined current capacity [8]; (2) Evaluated future needs for expansion [9]; (3) Created brainstormed alternatives; (4) Assessed the technical and financial feasibility of alternatives [10]; (5) Selected the most appropriate alternative; (6) Implemented this alternative as the future drew closer; (7) Evaluated the plant drawings and Identified operational bottlenecks [11]; (8) Scheduled non-bottleneck operations [12]; (9) Determined optimal operating levels [13]; (10) Maximized the use of operational bottlenecks [14]; *Location*: (1) Determined the best location to build our facilities [15] bearing in mind the company's strategy, strengths, weaknesses and characteristics of both clientele and supply chain; (2) Evaluated the suitability of already existing facilities [16]; (3) Closed down facilities [17]; (4) Opened facilities [18]; *Facility layout*: (1) Determined the most effective facility layout [19]; (2) Evaluated precedence diagrams [20]; (3) Estimated delays [21]; (4) Minimized transportation costs [22] and (5) Deemed multiple criteria in facility design [23]

Products: (1) Formulated quality goals [24]; (2) Set cost targets [25]; (3) Built and Tested prototypes [26]; (4) Translated product specifications into procedures, processes and work instructions [27]; (5) Carried out reverse engineering [28]; (6) Determined the most appropriate level of standardization [29]; (7) Compared design for manufacturing with design for assembly [30]; (8) Quantified reliability [31]; (9) Manufactured reliable products [32]; (10) Stored raw materials and outputs [33]; (11) Estimated the best quantity of inputs to store [34]; (12) Protected the company against suppliers' price fluctuations [35]; (13) Determined reordering timings; (14) Forecast demand; (15) Agreed upon lead times [36]; (16) Listed inventory items in order of priority [37]; (17) Developed master schedules [38]; (18) Created a final product structure tree [39]; (19) Determined the most adequate lot sizes [40]; (20) Fostered a green mindset to the entire supply chain [41]; (21) Evaluated and Certified suppliers [42]; (22) Bought raw materials; (23) Shortened the supply chain [43]; (24) Assessed and Mitigated supply chain risks [44]; (25) Coordinated purchasing logistics [45] and (26) Evaluated suppliers' policies on returned items [46]

Process: _Planning_: (1) Formulated and Solved linear programming models [47]; (2) Defined objective functions [48]; (3) Selected decision variables [49]; (4) Determined model constraints [50]; (5) Summarized in a spreadsheet expected payoffs for a myriad of operational processes [51]; (6) Created decision trees to evaluate alternatives and their consequences [52]; (7) Selected the process type presenting highest payoff for decisions made under certainty [53]; (8) Researched on strategies to deal with uncertainty [54]; (9) Assessed potential machinery; _Execution_: (1) Programmed equipment to carry out activities; (2) Designed jobs [55]; (3) Created self-directed teams [56]; (4) Evaluated furniture ergonomics [57]; (5) Bettered working conditions [58]; (6) Developed performance-enhancing incentives [59]; (7) Reduced job time per unit by X% as the number of repetitions increased; (8) Calculated time reductions; _Just in time_: (1) Implemented a just in time [60] approach to inventory; (2) Used near-by located suppliers [61]; _Lean operations_: (1) Used minimal resources and Produced high-quality goods and services [62]; (2) Reduced wastes [63]; (3) Improved the process continuously [64]; (4) Kept minimal inventory [65]; (5) Matched output with demand [66]; (6) Fostered a lean culture [67]; (7) Automated production; (8) Made the system flexible to accommodate required changes [68]; _Schedules_: (1) Scheduled operations and equipment use

[69]; (2) Created schedule charts [70]; (3) Controlled inputs and outputs [71]; (4) Calculated the number of jobs [72]; (5) Reduced scheduling problems [73]; (6) Provided immediate equipment repair upon breakdowns [74] and (7) Carried out preventive maintenance [75]

Quality: *Management*: (1) Interviewed end-users and Defined quality aspects from their viewpoint [76]; (2) Balanced the costs required to reach the defined quality standard [77]; (3) Priced products to account for quality requirements and Got approval from end-users; (4) Trained employees on quality drivers [78]; (5) Submitted cases and Won quality awards [79]; (6) Enhanced quality continuously [80]; (7) Carried out value-added benchmarking [81]; (8) Evaluated suppliers [82]; (9) Implemented approaches to improve operational efficiency and effectiveness [83]; (10) Created checking lists and control charts [84]; (11) Researched on the root causes of encountered problems [85]; *Control*: (1) Monitored processes [86]; (2) Scheduled inspections [87]; (3) Sampled and Inspected inputs and outputs for defects [88]; (4) Set limit targets for measures' variability [89]; (5) Took corrective actions to deal with defects and (6) Reduced the number of defects per unit by X%

Projects: (1) Evaluated and Selected projects [90]; (2) Defined project teams [91]; (3) Planned and Scheduled activities [92]; (4) Allocated resources [93]; (5) Created network precedence diagrams [94]; (6) Determined the critical path [95]; (7) Estimated times for activities [96]; (8) Identified, Assessed and Mitigated risks; (9) Monitored projects [97] and (10) Researched on the effectiveness of projects after they took place

Services: (1) Carried out a cost-benefit analysis for service capacity [98]; (2) Selected the number of tellers [99]; (3) Determined service time [100]; (4) Limited waiting-line length [101]; (5) Increased processing rate by X% and (6) Motivated customers to come at off-peak periods [102]

3.7. Negotiation

The present section of the chapter deals with the professional accomplishments related to Negotiation, which involves meeting interests and reaching agreements with other stakeholders:

NEGOTIATION:

Planning: *Being invited to negotiate*: (1) Inquired about the subject of the negotiation; (2) Decided whether or not to negotiate [1]; *Inviting to negotiate*: (1) Defined the scope of the negotiation; (2) Analyzed several feasible first offers to make [2]; (3) Selected the most appropriate one; (4) Assessed whether the other side would or would not be willing to negotiate; *Both cases*: (1) Assessed how important to our organization the other party is [3]; (2) Brainstormed all possible interests from both parties [4]; (3) Listed our interests in order of priority [5]; (4) Established a possible order for the other party's interests [6]; (5) Determined the most beneficial outcome for our company to look for [7]; (6) Gathered information from several sources in order to make well-grounded decisions [8]; (7) Deemed possible values for uncertain data [9]; (8) Determined our preferred schedules and those of the other party [10]; (9) Analyzed our risk-taking profile and that of the other side; (10) Determined which concessions our company could make and what concessions we would ask in exchange for them [11]; (11) Increased the number of issues to be negotiated [12]; (12) Identified ethical issues that may arise during the negotiation [13]; (13) Created solutions for them [14]; (14) Created from the scratch possible outcomes for the negotiation [15]; (15) Rated them according to the their ability to the meet both parties' most important interests [16]; (16) Decided how far in the negotiation we could go and (17) Selected to propose the value-added outcome that we think would best solve the pending issues [17]

Execution: *Being invited to negotiate*: (1) Ignored any unfair anchors [18]; (2) Responded with a feasible offer [19]; (3) Asked the other side to clarify his main interests [20]; *Inviting to negotiate*: (1) Made an anchored offer [21]; (2) Justified our offer [22]; *Both cases*: (1) Analyzed and Replied to subsequent offers made by the other party [23]; (2) Helped the other side identify many of his interests that our company could meet [24]; (3) Proposed solutions for ethical problems [25]; (4) Demonstrated that our company is as powerful as the other party [26]; (5) Took control of the discussion; (6) Showed knowledge of relevant technical data; (7) Calculated values mentally; (8) Told that the other side is important to our company [27]; (9) Told the other side that it is difficult for our company to make the concessions we are making [28]; (10) Determined my own and Guessed the other side's assumptions [29]; (11) Shared information on our interests [30]; (12) Kept secret some information [31]; (13) Adjusted and Showed the planned value-added outcome for both parties [32]; (14) Detected lies [33]; (15) Told indirectly the other party what could not be told directly [34]; (16) Proposed contingency clauses to contracts to manage upcoming uncertain events [35]; (17) Postponed difficult decisions [36] and (18) Reflected more deeply on them [37]

Control: *Both being invited to negotiate and inviting to negotiate*: (1) Rated the negotiation outcome [38]; (2) Identified mistakes [39]; (3) Brainstormed feasible corrections to the mistakes [40]; (4) If possible, Corrected the mistakes after the negotiation was held; (5) If not possible, Mitigated their consequences; (6) Evaluated the underlying reasons for the occurrence of the mistakes [41] and (7) Prepared better for upcoming negotiations [42]

3.8.Marketing

This section of the chapter deals with the Professional accomplishments in Marketing, which incorporate activities such as commercial planning of products and services, making them available in the consumer market and the evaluation of this process:

MARKETING:

Strategic Planning: (1) Formalized the organization mission, objectives, targets and business portfolio [1]; (2) Defined the survival strategy and the growth strategy [2]; (3) Defined budgets and controls [3] and (4) Built charts with variables related to marketing efforts [4]

Analysis: *External environment*: (1) Carried out the SWOT analysis for company's main products [5]; *Research*: (1) Created the company's marketing information system [6]; (2) Collected secondary information [7]; (3) Analyzed and Made decisions based on the available information [8]; *Consumer Behavior*: (1) Determined the factors that drive attitude modification regarding brands [9]; (2) Determined purchasing behavior [10]; (3) Determined the searched benefits at purchases [11]; (4) Determined which price reduction would cause a brand shift; (5) Determined the price increases that loyal customers tolerate; (6) Determined the image of competing brand according to customers; *Demand*: (1) Measured the current demand [12]; (2) Determined the market potential for the company's main products and markets [13]; (3) Forecast the future demand [14]; *Market Segmentation*: (1) Identified target markets [15]; (2) Selected target markets [16]; (3) Developed adequate products and marketing compounds [17]; (4) Proceeded to market segmentation [18]; (5) Measured the segment attractiveness [19] and (6) Developed a positioning for each target segment [20]

Product: (1) Defined the basic and additional benefits of the company's products [21]; (2) Established quality standards of products to go on and buy from suppliers; (3) Selected products to present a line of products [22]; (4) Classified products by purchasing habits [23]; (5) Defined the value to the client of the products that the company sells compared to those that competitors do [24]; (6) Identified differences among products that benefit our company [25]; (7) Created defensive brands and attack brands [26]; (8) Associated values to the company's brands [27]; (9) Carried out the marketing commercial and strategic analysis of new products [28]; (10) Enhanced products according to information on customers' needs [29] and (11) Carried out quality tests in the customers' facilities

Price: *Price Setting*: (1) Defined the pricing policy of the company [30]; (2) Set prices based on a myriad of factors and time horizons [31]; (3) Searched for products with high price-elasticity of demand for price reductions and low price-elasticity of demand for price increases; (4) Set prices for product launching [32]; (5) Practiced discounts and promotional prices in exchange for desirable attitudes of the clients [33]; (6) Set referential prices in the consumers' minds [34]; (7) Carried out an attitude change among customers regarding the price of products; *Price Variations*: (1) Increased and Decreased prices for a series of plausible reasons [35]; (2) Explained these reasons persuasively to clients [36]; (3) Kept prices at a satisfactory level in order not to attract new entrants; (4) Widespread among clients saving methods; (5) Dealt with client and competitor reactions to our price modifications [37]; (6) Monitored competitor's price changes [38] and (7) Avoided a price war [39]

Place: *Distribution Channels*: (1) Added more channels to the company's hybrid marketing system [40]; (2) Collected from the distribution channels information on the end users [41]; (3) Solved horizontal and vertical conflicts [42]; (4) Determined which value each channel should provide [43]; (5) Conducted cooperated advertising with suppliers and distributors [44]; *Logistics*: (1) Defined the logistic objectives [45]; (2) Planned the sales and purchasing logistics of the company [46]; (3) Made agreements with transportation firms; (4) Planned the warehousing [47] and sorting of products; (5) Defined return policies; (6) Researched on the importance of distribution services in order to establish their desirable levels; (7) Shared with stakeholders information on logistics [48]; *Retail*: (1) Used retailers as intermediaries when convenient [49]; *Wholesale*: (1) Established representation partnerships [50]; (2) Helped wholesale clients to define their position regarding the acquired products [51] and (3) Used wholesalers as intermediaries when required [52]

Promotion: _Advertising_: (1) Established the advertising objectives [53]; (2) Defined the target audience [54]; (3) Defined the budget [55]; (4) Created messages [56]; (5) Selected the media [57]; (6) Executed the message [58]; (7) Decided on the media chronology [59]; (8) Evaluated the advertising effort [60]; (9) Announced the company's products in a website for industrial suppliers and in magazines of industrial circulation; (10) Launched and Updated the company internet website; (11) Synchronized the marketing mix to conduct integrated communications [61]; _Sales Promotion_: (1) Established the Sales promotion objectives [62]; (2) Selected tools [63]; (3) Developed and Implemented the Sales promotion program [64]; (4) Defined the budget [65]; (5) Evaluated the Sales promotion program [66]; _Public Relations_: (1) Was nominated the company's press assessor; (2) Chose public relations tools [67]; (3) Established objectives [68]; (4) Selected messages and vehicles [69]; (5) Created news and events [70]; (6) Executed the public relations plan [71] and (7) Evaluated the outcome [72]

Customer Relationship Management: (1) Developed a portfolio of X thousand potential clients worldwide and presented the company; (2) Y thousand clients replied asking for quotations; (3) Followed up regular customers; (4) In X trips, Conducted and Wrote up reports on meetings with Y companies in X cities (Y countries); (5) Expanded the sales in X countries (Y clients), generating $ X millions of operational revenue through Y purchase orders thanks to X companies from this portfolio; (6) Managed the sales team and Trained the team [73] to avoid marketing myopia; (7) Provided technical assistance; (8) Reactivated clients, Identified the reasons why we lost them and Eliminated or Reduced the objections [74]; (9) Segmented the market according to the profitability that the client brings to the company and (10) Conceded financial and social benefits to clients [75]

Competitors: (1) Identified the company's competitors [76]; (2) Determined the size of the market and respective participation share for our main products [77]; (3) Determined the objectives, strengths and weaknesses of the competitors and Monitored their actions [78]; (4) Carried out benchmarking; (5) Used attack and defense strategies and (6) Split the attention between clients and competitors [79]

Global Market: (1) Thought in global terms regarding importation, exportation, manufacturing, purchasing and sales, looking for international and domestic advantages [80]; (2) Developed regional partnerships [81] and (3) Decided in how many and which countries to operate as well as Offered an adapted marketing mix [82]

Services: (1) Trained the customer-contact staff to perform a high-level interactive marketing [83] and in this way generate bilateral satisfaction and (2) Added tangibility to the services developed to clients and employees [84]

Ethics: (1) Defined the corporate policy regarding advertising standards [85]; (2) Established a customer channel for suggestions and complaints and (3) Promoted internal and external marketing

3.9.Foreign Trade

This section of the chapter is devoted to professional accomplishments regarding Foreign Trade, encompassing sales and purchases from overseas companies:

FOREIGN TRADE:

Strategic Management: (1) Developed the company policy, including all critical aspects to international commerce [1]; (2) Kept updated with domestic and overseas' legislation [2]; (3) Balanced the advantages and disadvantages of importing/exporting against domestic sales/purchases [3]; (4) Gathered global marketplace data (importers, exporters, prices, quantities, dates) regarding our most important products; (5) Created standard operations' procedures [4] and Considered them as benchmarks; (6) Upon expected annual requirements, Prepared the department budget [5] and (7) Rated carriers and forwarders according to critical criteria in order to select the most suitable ones [6]

Operations: (1) Evaluated the most appropriate Incoterm for each shipment [7]; (2) Used appropriate and agreed upon HS codes to declare goods [8]; (3) Analyzed the tradeoffs between ocean and air freight [9]; (4) Followed up shipments and (5) Created a checklist to pay attention to points that can lead to a red flag for shipments undergoing customs clearance [10]

Imports: (1) Made sure the overseas suppliers are sound companies [11]; (2) Concluded (in loco as far as possible) that suppliers can manufacture the product we are importing according to agreed standards [12]; (3) Had a step supplier [13] for the event of a manufacturing or exporting difficulty; (4) Dealt with exclusivity issues [14]; (5) Signed an arbitration agreement [15]; (6) Performed extensive laboratory tests with samples [16]; (7) Selected suppliers that possess the ISO9001 certification [17]; (8) Set packing and labeling standards [18]; (9) Created a cost spreadsheet for all incurred costs in order to calculate selling prices [19]; (10) Built a checklist on desired qualities to rate foreign factories and select the most suitable ones; (11) Acknowledged the supplier is willing to visit our company [20]; (12) Chose suppliers that met security and compliance laws that have a clear policy on returns [21]; (13) Requested shipping documents first by email to check for omissions and misstatements, Corrected them if any [22] and thereafter Requested by courier multiple comprehensive sets of them (certificates of origin, commercial invoice, packing list, bill of lading or airway bill, quality certificate and sanitary certificate); (14) Kept all commitments in writing; (15) Brought in competitors; (16) Negotiated international freight rates; (17) Established relationship first, before purchase and (18) Developed a import notification process to validate shipments as authentic [23]

Exports: (1) Developed and Used a supply chain management checklist containing relevant foreign trade operational aspects; (2) Issued shipping documents (proforma invoice, commercial invoice, packing list and quality certificate); (3) Got other parties to issue other documents (bill of lading or airway bill, certificates of origin and sanitary certificate), Forwarded them to the importer for checking and accepting purposes and then Sent by courier multiple comprehensive sets of them; (4) Familiar with the various types of drawback [24]; (5) Identified drawback opportunities [25]; (6) Requested our customers abroad to check for the local need of import licenses to import the goods we are offering [26]; (7) Presented and Retained export licenses whenever there was a customs' demand; (8) Familiarized with equipment, procedures and training required to conduct security screening [27]; (9) Assessed expected costs and revenues that would result from carrying out screening procedures in our factory [28]; (10) Reduced average delivery times by X days and Lowered costs by X%; (11) Regarding credit terms, Provided higher price and extended payment terms to tapper markets that otherwise would refuse to negotiate with our organization; (12) Created a portfolio of clients that contacted our factory and were willing to buy our products and Forwarded this list to regular importers and distributors, when these clients were small and belonged to their regions; (13) Ran product seminars and sales campaigns [29] and (14) Developed an international business network

Human Resources: (1) Attracted and Retained all rounders in the foreign trade labor market [30]; (2) Compensated commensurate with performance [31]; (3) Offered international trips with offspring during school vacations [32]; (4) Provided high level continuing education [33]; (5) Motivated with profit-sharing incentives [34]; (6) Created clear-cut pathways for growth and promotion [35] and (7) Sent key employees to attend international conferences to do networking [36]

Risk management: (1) Identified and Assessed potential risk exposures [37]; (2) Determined which risks were most likely to occur; (3) Evaluated loss control options [38]; (4) Issued a company policy against terrorism [39]; (5) Carried out an internal audit on security issues; (6) Contracted insurance policies to mitigate the most prominent risks [40]; (7) Diversified countries and goods to do business with [41]; (8) Balanced insurable interests and cost of premiums [42]; (9) Wrote up a contingency plan for unexpected operational and non-operational events [43] and (10) Notified immediately the authorities upon suspicious occurrences

Compliance: (1) Carried out internal compliance management audits [44]; (2) Monitored compliance measures [45]; (3) Retained documents for all shipments for X years; (4) Dealt with government institutions involved in international trade; (5) Developed guidelines to cope with a customs broker audit [46] and (6) Wrote up a compliance manual addressing all relevant issues [47]

3.10.Supply Management

The professional activities regarding the Supply Management subject comprise managing suppliers and executing sourcing strategies for products used all over the organization.

SUPPLY MANAGEMENT:

Strategy: (1) Developed the organization's policy regarding sourcing [1]; (2) Set a global sourcing program [2]; (3) Integrated electronically the main partners pertaining to our supply chain [3]; (4) Centralized the coordination of the sourcing program [4] and (5) Decentralized the execution of operational transactions [5]

Purchasing Routine: (1) Created a purchasing procedure manual [6]; (2) Gathered specifications [7]; (3) Forecast quantities [8]; (4) Issued purchase orders; (5) Scheduled delivery [9]; (6) Received goods; (7) Paid invoices [10]; (8) Kept records of all transactions for X years; (9) Decreased the time between need recognition and receipt of goods by Y% and (10) Carried out reverse auctions [11]

Supplier selection: (1) Identified potential suppliers [12]; (2) Defined the methodology for supplier evaluation [13]; (3) Evaluated suppliers [14]; (4) Determined a scoring system for supplier selection [15]; (5) Added X new suppliers to the company; (6) Categorized suppliers as they would serve for habitual or single purchases [16]; (7) Established preferred suppliers for each product [17]; (8) Disqualified suppliers [18]; (9) Managed supplier risk [19] and (10) Followed up the entire supply base [20]

Commodities: (1) Negotiated purchase prices, delivery and payment terms [21] and quality; (2) Added X new items to the company's product line; (3) Reduced Y thousand dollars in importation costs; (4) Gathered stakeholders' requirements for products and services [22]; (5) Calculated consumption rates [23]; (6) Reduced the levels of inventory required by the company's several departments [24]; (7) Lowered raw material inventories to Y days' supply; (8) Created an annual suppliers' meeting; (9) Informed suppliers about our current supply challenges; (10) Awarded golden plates to suppliers in recognition of better supply conditions and (11) Developed a supply chain virtual portal [25]

Supplier quality: (1) Shared with our Chinese suppliers our expectations [26] about specifications; (2) Improved the quality of our Chinese suppliers; (3) Monitored supplier quality [27]; (4) Emphasized prevention of defects [28]; (5) Determined the cost of quality [29]; (6) Invited key suppliers to participate in product and process development [30] and (7) Proposed an innovation that bettered supplier quality and saved time and money

Logistics: (1) Developed a transportation strategy [31]; (2) Identified key transportation performance variables [32]; (3) Selected transportation modes [33]; (4) Selected carriers [34]; (5) Managed indirect expenses [35] and (6) Saved X thousand dollars with better transportation options

Overseas sourcing: (1) Hired X global sourcing managers to work in Y major cities worldwide; (2) Considered the suppliers' culture [36]; (3) Developed a sourcing strategy to support X overseas factories for Y kinds of commodities; (4) Developed more than one supplier for each commodity [37]; (5) Enhanced bargaining power; (6) Mitigated potential risks [38]; (6) Selected the most appropriate currency for each deal [39] and (7) Honed own cross-functional and cross-cultural negotiation skills

Long-term Contracts: (1) Selected contract types [40]; (2) Negotiated contract elements [41]; (3) Analyzed breaches of contracts; (4) Created escape clauses [42]; (5) Evaluated expressed and implied warranties [43]; (6) Set contingency clauses for unforeseen events [44]; (7) Researched on the supplier financial situation [45] and (8) Signed contracts electronically [46]

Ethics: (1) Created a code of ethics for the purchasing function [47]; (2) Informed the supply manager about responsibilities and liabilities [48]; (3) Monitored the entire supply chain to prevent frauds [49]; (4) Protected trade secrets [50]; (5) Avoided reciprocity [51]; (6) Trained staff on ethical issues [52]; (7) Kept records and reports on unethical behavior [53] and (8) Established limits of authority [54]

Control: (1) Measured purchasing and supply performance [55]; (2) Aligned the supply chain measurement system with the organization's goals and other departments [56]; (3) Established a quality enhancement procedure based on defective parts per million [57]; (4) Focused on both short-term and long-term performance measures [58]; (5) Provided performance feedback [59] and (6) Carried out performance benchmarking [60]

3.11.Human Resources

Human Resources encompass managing people jobs, from fulfilling vacancies to rewarding performance. In the lines that follow, the professional activities on this subject are presented:

HUMAN RESOURCES:

Strategy: (1) Developed the organizational policy on HR [1]; (2) Restructured the HR department according to the state-of-the-practice; (3) During my tenure, the company was shortlisted to the award 'The best companies to work for' (http://fortune.com/best-companies) for X consecutive years and (4) Increased employee retention

Planning: (1) Carried out a Jobs & Skills Audit [2]; (2) Planned the succession of key employees [3]; (3) Re-designed old jobs and Designed new jobs [4]; (4) Carried out job satisfaction [5] surveys and (5) Involved the organization in a cause employees value high [6]

Metrics: (1) Created HR metrics in the four areas of the balanced scorecard [7]; (2) Calculated and Evaluated Strategic and Operational HR measures [8]; (3) Carried out internal HR audits [9] and external benchmarking analysis [10]

Recruiting: (1) Recruited X candidates; (2) Developed a recruiting strategy [11] and long-range plans [12]; (3) Cultivated networks to generate pool of applicants [13]; (4) Built employment branding [14] in the worldwide labor market; (5) Posted job advertisements [15]; (6) Selected recruiting messages [16]; (7) Evaluated recruiting metrics [17] and (8) Participated at job fairs [18]

Selecting: (1) Received X applications; (2) Interviewed Y applicants; (3) Created and Administered tests [19]; (4) Conducted background investigation [20]; (5) Placed X employees; (6) Coordinated follow-up of these employees; (7) Maintained appropriate records and reports [21] and (8) Researched on the effectiveness of the selection process [22]

Training: (1) Developed strategic training plans [23]; (2) Evaluated the training process [24]; (3) Considered multiple learning styles [25]; (4) Selected training methodologies [26]; (5) Provided reinforcement and feedback after training [27] and (6) Conducted the welcoming and orientation meeting of new staff

Career Development: (1) Formulated a career development strategy [28] and Forwarded to the employees; (2) Established a career development center [29]; (3) Issued an HR newsletter; (4) Practiced self-development and (5) Coached and Developed a successor and subordinates [30]

Performance: (1) Supervised employees [31]; (2) Selected appraisal methods [32]; (3) Communicated expected performance levels [33]; (4) Compared them against benchmarks; (5) Measured and Communicated employees performance timely [34]; (6) Provided intrinsic and extrinsic rewards [35] and (7) Linked employees' key performance indicators to organizational performance measures [36]

Compensating: (1) Gathered data on pay surveys [37]; (2) Determined pay structures and increases [38] and (3) Decided onto pay secrecy [39]

Safety: (1) Was nominated safety officer; (2) Created safety policies [40]; (3) Carried out safety audits [41]; (4) Researched on the cause of accidents [42]; (5) Communicated hazards and emergency procedures [43]; (6) Translated X foreign manufacturers' products Materials Safety Datasheets; (7) Managed ergonomics programs [44] and (8) Kept safety records for inspection [45]

Health: (1) Created a wellness leaflet [46] and (2) Forwarded it to new employees

Security Management: (1) Monitored employees' computers in real-time [47]; (2) Subscribed magazines on workplace violence [48]; (3) Created a violence response team [49] and (4) Carried out annual security audits [50]

Labor relations: (1) Created policies on employees' rights [51]; (2) Kept warnings' and suspensions' records [52]; (3) Conducted exit interviews [53] and (4) Coordinated discussions with syndicates [54]

3.12.Organizational Behavior

The professional activities concerning the subject Organizational Behavior involve dealing with people and motivating them to do their best to achieve established goals:

ORGANIZATIONAL BEHAVIOR:

Planning: (1) Honed own leadership skills [1]; (2) Assessed staff core values [2] and (3) Researched on the impact that individuals, teams and organizational structure have on behavior [3]

Emotions: (1) Fostered positive emotions and moods [4]; (2) Understood employees' emotional cues [5]; (3) Identified and Modified own emotions; (4) Rewarded organizational citizenship behavior [6]; (5) Evaluated events after they took place [7] and (6) Created an open dialogue to deal with anger

Personality: *Candidates*: (1) Measured personality [8]; (2) Classified candidates according to their personality type [9]; (3) Ranked candidates' values in terms of their intensity [10]; (4) Preferred candidates that demonstrated career loyalty; (5) Assessed candidate-job fit [11] and *Own*: (1) Clarified about own individual dimensions of culture

Perception: (1) Determined the influence of situations on perception [12]; (2) Evaluated potential internal and external reasons leading to success and failure [13]; (3) Summarized people by multiple factors; (4) Gathered several viewpoints to solve pending issues and (5) Justified decisions

Motivation: (1) Hired people that identified with jobs [14]; (2) Hired people whose performance underpinned their self-worth [15]; (3) Empowered employees to define tasks [16]; (4) Improved working conditions; (5) Motivated staff to better their performance [17]; (6) Raised employees' job satisfaction [18] and (8) Combined extrinsic with intrinsic rewards [19]

Teams: (1) Formed teams [20]; (2) Defined objectives [21]; (3) Set timetables; (4) Distributed jobs; (5) Fostered intra-group support; (6) Rewarded both individuals and the group as a whole [22]; (7) Shared information [23]; (8) Generated ideas [24]; (9) Coordinated projects, (10) Provided equipment [25]; (11) Planned activities and (12) Solved conflicts [26]

Communication: (1) Shaped messages according to employees' cultural context [27]; (2) Defined social media policies [28]; (3) Motivated staff to become my social media followers; (4) Monitored employees' use of social media [29] to identify the release of confidential information [30]; (5) Researched on the character of job candidates in the social media [31] and (6) Monitored outbound email messages from employees [32]

Leadership: (1) Inspired the staff toward achieving goals [33]; (2) Oversaw jobs; (3) Streamlined my role as a leader; (4) Organized work; (5) Met deadlines; (6) Established mutual respect with subordinates [34]; (7) Helped with problems; (8) Looked at old problems in new ways [35] and (9) Trained staff to carry out activities independently [36]

Negotiation: (1) Developed consensus over job tasks and goals; (2) Motivated employees to help one another; (3) Prepared for discussions [37]; (4) Satisfied our interests and those of the other side [38]; (5) Justified points of view [39]; (6) Agreed and Disagreed as required and (7) Carried out intercultural negotiations [40]

Organizing: (1) Designed the organizational chart [41]; (2) Created departments [42]; (3) Separated jobs [43]; (4) Clarified reporting relationships [44]; (5) Closed locations; (6) Reduced staff and (7) Balanced the need to foster creativity in a decentralized control manner with the need for controlling the company's destiny in a centralized control manner [45]

<u>Culture</u>: (1) Developed and Cultivated a positive organizational culture [46]; (2) Fostered our core values and beliefs across the company [47]; (3) Established a culture-process fit organization-wide; (4) Determined the most important goals and key staff members to reach them [48] and (5) Emphasized hard word toward company growth

<u>Human resources</u>: (1) Identified candidates well suited to jobs [49]; (2) Carried out cognitive ability and personality tests [50]; (3) Invited employees to take part at training workshops [51]; (4) Recognized employees' outstanding performance [52]; (5) Developed careers [53]; (6) Justified each one's performance appraisal [54] and (7) Decreased absenteeism and turnover

<u>Organizational change</u>: (1) Carried out planned changes [55]; (2) Dealt with resistance to change [56]; (3) Stated the reason for change [57]; (4) Researched what else would require change within the organization; (5) Created a culture of innovation and learning [58]; (6) Evaluated potential sources of stress [59] and (7) Mitigated stress generation [60]

3.13.Accounting

The professional accomplishments regarding Accounting derive from the assessment of relationships among managerial variables pertaining to reports (such as the financial statement) and the seizure of business opportunities:

ACCOUNTING:

Planning: _General_: (1) Planned the future investing and financing activities; (2) Identified demanders of accounting reports [1]; (3) Evaluated users' information requirements [2]; (4) Made accounting reports for users [3]; (5) Analyzed financial statements [4]; (6) Adapted the financial statement to forward to banks, creditors [5] and owners; (7) Detected accounting errors in accounting reports [6]; (8) Requested their correction; (9) Researched on the underlying reasons for outcomes [7]; (10) Compared our financial results with those of market leaders both countrywide and worldwide [8]; (11) Defined policies for future actions; _Depreciation_: (1) Compared methods used to compute depreciation [9]; (2) Selected one of them; (3) Decided on the lifetime of fixed assets [10]; (4) Sold fixed assets for a value superior to their cost after depreciation; _Receivables_: (1) Selected an estimation method for uncollectibles [11] and (2) Estimated uncollectibles [12]

Software: (1) Compared top-tier accounting software; (2) Listed the modules required for the accounting system; (3) Decided which internal controls would be desirable from the stakeholders' standpoint and (4) Implemented the software [13]

Payroll: (1) Collected input data for the payroll system [14]; (2) Computed employee net pay [15]; (3) Disbursed payroll [16]; (4) Designed internal controls for payroll systems [17] and (5) Forecast requirements for contingent liabilities [18]

Control: (1) Created accounting control policies [19] and procedures [20]; (2) Monitored internal controls [21]; (3) Researched on the causes underlying financial results; (4) Decided what information to report to shareholders; (5) Assessed risks [22]; (6) Separated responsibilities for interrelated tasks [23]; (7) Used authorization as a security measure [24]; (8) Pre-numbered documents [25]; (9) Located weaknesses; (10) Checked bank statements [26] and (11) Controlled cash all its way through [27]

Managerial Accounting: *Rises*: From the fiscal year of my enrolment to the company management till the current fiscal year, Increased the following financial variables and ratios [28] (percentage between parentheses): Net income (X%); Liquidity (Y%); Solvency (X%); Working capital (Y%); Current ratio (X%); Revenue (Y%); Gross profit (X%); Selling price (Y%); Quick ratio (X%); Accounts receivable turnover (Y%); Sales to assets (X%); Earnings per share (Y%); Dividends per share (X%); Net profit (Y%); Inventory turnover (X%); Revenue per employee (Y%); Fixed assets turnover (X%); *Falls*: For the past X years, Managed cross-functional teams and Lowered the following financial ratios and variables [29] (percentage between parentheses): Liabilities to owners' equity (Y%); Production costs (X%); Factory overhead (Y%); Office overhead (X%); Uncollectible accounts expenses (Y%); Number of days' sales in receivables (X%); Number of days' sales in inventory (Y%) and Accounts payable (X%)

Partnerships: (1) Compared legal forms for organizing and operating businesses [30]; (2) Selected one of them; (3) Set a date for IPO; (4) Admitted partners to our business [31]; (5) Created clauses in the social contract for withdrawal terms of a partner [32]; (6) Dealt with the death of a partner [33] and (7) Liquidated a partnership [34]

Investments: (1) Bought X% of stakes of the main competitors and partners in the supply chain; (2) Reinvested in current operations cash drawn from the company's regular operations [35]; (3) Carried out temporary investments [36]; (4) Carried out long-term investments [37] in stock of other companies; (5) Bought Y% of stakes of non-competitors and non-partners in the supply chain; (6) Consolidated with competitors and partners in the supply chain [38]; (7) Calculated the dividend yield [39]; (8) Explained to shareholders the company's policy on dividends [40]

Sales' analysis: (1) Established the relationship between sales revenue and costs [41]; (2) Determined how many units of production output must our company sell to break even [42]; (3) Identified the activities that cause the cost to change [43]; (4) Classified costs as either variable or fixed [44]; (5) Analyzed the effects of changes in selling prices on profits [45]; (6) Analyzed the effects of changes in costs on profits [46]; (7) Carried out decisions of whether to lease or to sell [47]; (8) Discontinued a product; (9) Carried out decisions of whether to make or to buy [48]; (10) Estimated activity costs [49]; (11) Assigned responsibility for cost and profit centers [50]; (12) Evaluated manufacturing costs by comparing actual with expected results [51]; (13) Considered decentralizing operations [52]; (14) Evaluated alternative proposals for long-term investments in fixed assets [53]; (15) Determined the amount of output required to cover operating expenses and (16) Calculated operational and financial budgets [54]

Capital investments: (1) Compared initial costs of long-term capital investments to their future earnings and cash flows [55]; (2) Determined the useful life of capital investment proposals [56] and (3) Considered uncertainties [57]

3.14. Credit Management

Credit Management stands for activities such as assessing creditworthiness and collecting cash. Following are presented the professional accomplishments regarding this business subject:

CREDIT MANAGEMENT:

Strategy: Defined a credit management policy for the company [1]

Planning: (1) Integrated sales and credit departments [2]; (2) Educated the customer about payment terms [3]; (3) Got customers' credit information at early negotiation stages [4]; (4) Defined the shortest and the longest credit terms and further conditions of sale to be applied for incoming domestic sales [5] and (5) Created and Handed out to sales and credit staff a leaflet about the likely behavior of defaulting clients [6]

Risk Assessment: (1) Analyzed banks', suppliers' and customers' creditworthiness reports issued by credit assessment organizations and (2) Defined the currencies our company should use to import and those to be used to export [7]

Measurement: (1) Established a method to rate the creditworthiness of new and existing clients [8]; (2) Established cash targets [9]; (3) Calculated and Reduced by X% the overall customers default measure; (4) Requested from new customers their financial statements and P&L statements [10]; (5) Calculated insolvency predictors of these customers [11]; (6) Showed to our banks and foreign suppliers that our financial statements indicate our acceptable solvency and (7) Controlled the reports produced by the sales ledger staff [12]

Collection: (1) Decided which collection techniques to employ in a case-by-case approach [13]; (2) Trained the collection staff how to prepare telephone collection calls in advance and how to cope with the main excuses used by debtor through telephone [14]; (3) Congratulated staff members that succeeded in recovering debts [15]; (4) Analyzed underlying reasons of failing staff members [16] and (5) From time to time and for the largest debts, Used external collection agencies [17]

Credit Insurance: (1) Requested a quotation of a credit insurance policy; (2) Carried out a cost-benefit analysis of the proposal [18]; (3) Decided to try out credit insurance for one fiscal year; (4) Evaluated the final outcome and (5) Decided whether or not to continue using credit insurance policies

Commercial Credit Law: (1) Followed up liquidation cases in which the company was a creditor and (2) Decided not to sue low value insolvents unless a collective legal process took place

Credit Services: (1) Carried out a cost-benefit analysis comparing internal cash collection against invoice financing, factoring and invoice discounting [19]; (2) Decided on the best alternative in financial terms [20] and (3) Established credit and debit cards as a new way of payment for the company's invoices [21]

3.15. Finance

The professional accomplishments of the subject Finance involve, among other issues, financing decisions in order to generate resources required to develop current and future activities:

FINANCE:

Investments: (1) Defined the company's policy on investments [1]; (2) Redistributed the resources across banks to reach the private banking status in the majority of them; (3) Determined the investor profile of the company owners; (4) Defined the budget available for investments; (5) Evaluated investment funds and (6) Built and efficient [2] and diversified portfolio of investments that yielded X% in Y months generating $ X millions

Debt: (1) Defined the company's policy on debt [3]; (2) Determined the ideal debt for several time horizons [4]; (3) Evaluated financing sources; (4) Decided between lending and borrowing money [5]; (5) Decided between issuing shares or borrowing money; (6) Calculated the total debt and total equity of the company; (7) Obtained higher interest when lending money than when borrowing money; (8) Paid debts and interest taxes on them and (9) Utilized fiscal benefits [6]

Dividends: (1) Defined the company's policy on dividends [7]; (2) Balanced between distributing dividends and reinvesting profits [8]; (3) Increased the dividends' value by X%; (4) Avoided sudden modifications in the dividends [9]; (5) Provided a fair level of dividends [10]; (6) Determined the objective in the long-run for the dividends' distribution index [11] and (7) Adapted the objectives for the dividends' distribution index to investment opportunities [12]

Planning: (1) Listed the financial needs [13]; (2) Defined origin and application of resources for several upcoming years [14]; (3) Prepared accounting reports [15]; (4) Generated resources [16]; (5) Defined inventory levels [17]; (6) Determined deadlines for clients' payments [18]; (7) Determined credit limits [19]; (8) Forecast the monthly cash flow for several years [20] and (9) Considered the integrated effect of investment and financing decisions

Risk: *Domestic*: (1) Identified and Classified risks [21]; (2) Analyzed risks [22]; (3) Decided which risks would be covered by an insurance policy and which would not [23]; (4) Built scenarios [24] resulting from the need of a risk coverage; (5) Evaluated the opportunity cost of capital [25]; *International*: (1) Evaluated investing overseas [26]; (2) Defined currencies to discount cash flows [27]; (3) Analyzed the currency exchange risk [28] and (4) Contracted an insurance policy for the most likely risks

Shares: (1) Maximized the company's share value [29]; (2) Estimated the average profit per share [30]; (3) Calculated the price of new shares [31]; (4) Sold out shares [32] and (5) Re-bought shares [33]

Capital opening: (1) Carried out an initial public offering of shares [34]; (2) Decided between a public subscription and a private placement [35]; (3) Selected subscripting individuals for the shares [36]; (4) Prepared a registration file [37]; (5) Set commissions [38]; (6) Estimated how much the investors were willing to pay for the new shares [39]; (7) Built a book with the potential purchase orders [40] and (8) Used this information to set the issuing price [41]

Obligations: (1) Evaluated obligations [42]; (2) Decided with which type of obligation to work [43]; (3) Amortized obligations [44]; (4) Modified the price of obligations [45]; (5) Took obligations out of circulation [46] and (6) Carried out a private placement of obligations [47]

Options: (1) Evaluated options [48]; (2) Sold out options [49]; (3) Bought options; (4) Conducted investing and financing decisions that included options [50]; (5) Calculated the price of options [51] and (6) Rewarded executives based on share options [52]

Valuation: (1) Evaluated how much our company was worth in case a horizontal or vertical acquisition would take place [53]; (2) Evaluated how much one of our business units was worth to put it on sale [54]; (3) Evaluated how much our company was worth in case it would open the capital [55]; (4) Decided between closing down the company and go on operating and (5) Sold the company

Real options: (1) Identified real options [56]; (2) Assessed variables relevant to real options [57]; (3) Carried out projects; (4) Conducted analysis of scenarios [58]; (5) Modified projects [59]; (6) Identified uncertainties [60]; (7) Abandoned projects temporarily or permanently [61]; (8) Established schedules for activities [62]; (9) Determined the duration of projects [63]; (10) Took corrective actions and (11) Assessed competitors' real options [64]

Leasing: (1) Evaluated leasing proposals [65]; (2) Decided between leasing and purchasing [66] and (3) Balanced fines and benefits of canceling contracts [67]

Mergers & Acquisitions: (1) Estimated whether potential mergers would produce greater profits than those accrued by each company separately [68]; (2) Conducted mergers [69]; (3) Sought undervalued companies in the business field [70]; (4) Purchased them; (5) Evaluated the economic gains in potential acquisitions [71]; (6) Carried out leveraged buyouts [72]; (7) Reduced wastes [73]; (8) Improved operational efficiency [74]; (8) Separated one business unit from the acquired company [75] and (9) Restructured and Sold out this unit [76]

3.16.Economics

The professional activities involved in the subject Economics deal with the company inserted in a market or industry context, where costs, quantities and profits result in prices and revenues:

ECONOMICS:

Micro-economics: *Production Costs*: (1) Calculated the total revenue, total cost and profit [1]; (2) Determined the implicit costs [2]; (3) Compared the economic profit with the accounting one [3]; (4) Built a production function of the company as a whole [4]; (5) Calculated the marginal product [5]; (6) Placed in a graph several cost curves (such as total, average, fixed, variable and marginal), both in the short and in the long-run [6]; (7) Transformed diseconomies of scale into economies of scale; *Externalities*: (1) Internalized the negative externality of production (industrial wastes) through the selective disposal and subsequent sale for waste recycling; (2) Promoted the sharing of foreign language and computer knowledge among employees as a positive externality resulting from long-term preparation and (3) Reduced the risk of strike as a negative externality by keeping the majority of new hires from universities, as in past occurrences this segment was less prone to join strikes; *Monopoly*: (1) Obtained patents over products that transformed the company in a monopoly [7]; (2) Maximized the monopoly profit [8]; (3) Evaluated the customers' willingness to pay [9]; (4) Selected criteria and Practiced price discrimination [10]; *Oligopoly*: (1) After playing several times the game of the prisoner's dilemma, Learned the competitors' tactics and Selected the most appropriate strategy [11] and *Monopolistic competition*: (1)

Announced products a little bit differentiated in order to avoid a price war

Macro-economics: *Gross Domestic Product*: (1) Elevated the productivity (and consequently the GDP) through employee training (increase of human capital), purchase of more commercial and industrial properties, Reading business best-seller books (improvement of technological know-how) and increase of inventory turnover; (2) Trained the employees about financial and family planning in order to stimulate savings, increase GDP per capita and increase living standards of all; (3) Corrected mistaken perceptions of clients regarding cost-benefit of products, stimulating the demand for products priced higher but that present longer useful life; *Unemployment*: (1) Lowered the unemployment rate once a year through the increase of the number of staff members from N to N/(1-u), where u = official unemployment rate, whenever the marginal profit of our products still kept positive; *Inflation*: (1) Lowered the inflation trying to purchase from wholesalers or manufacturers instead of from retailers whenever possible; (2) Lowered the shoe sole cost [12] through the increase of the minimum purchasing invoice value of the clients, so that they would make fewer visits to our company; (3) Lowered the menu cost [13] by keeping the company's price list with a slightly higher profitability to mitigate the need to update it constantly and (4) Specialized the company in what it makes best, that is, saving resources and maximizing the value to the client in a profitable manner

3.17.Insurance

The professional accomplishments of the Insurance business field deal with potential and incurred losses, and contracting insurance policies to transfer the risk, either partially or totally, to an insurer:

INSURANCE:

Ethics: (1) Kept all losses as accidental and unintentional [1]

Training: (1) Involved the staff in a loss prevention program of fire, explosion and employees' work-related injuries and diseases and (2) Educated employees on insurable and non-insurable risks

Planning: (1) Created an integrated risk management program [2]; (2) Identified loss exposures and the main assets to be protected [3]; (3) Classified risks by nature [4]; (4) Expressed the risk in monetary terms; (5) Compared techniques for treating loss exposures [5]; (6) Selected the most appropriate ones [6]; (7) Calculated the probability of losses [7]; (8) Avoided loss exposures [8]; (9) Combined loss exposures when risk could be reduced by doing so; (10) Designed production and delivery flowcharts; (11) Recorded historical loss data [9]; (12) Estimated the loss of business income in case of shutdown of our facilities; (13) Forecast the organization's upcoming losses [10] and (14) Modeled catastrophes [11]

Emergencies: (1) Established a contingency plan for the event of a shutdown of our factory; (2) Installed sprinkler systems for the event of a fire outburst [12] and (3) Bought alarm systems for the office and factory buildings

Execution: (1) Carried out physical inspections [13]; (2) Gathered proofs of loss [14]; (3) Reduced the severity of losses after they occurred [15]; (4) Reduced the frequency of particular losses [16]; (5) Resumed partial operations after the occurrence of losses and full operations within X years from that time; (6) Stabilized profits after a loss; (7) Continued growing the company after a loss took place; (8) Retained part or all of the losses stemming from a given loss [17]; (9) Paid losses; (10) Carried out contractual loss transfers [18]; (11) Monitored integrated risk management programs [19]; (12) Measured losses [20]; (13) Verified that a loss was covered by an insurance policy [21]; (14) Notified losses to claims adjustors [22]; (15) Claimed compensation for covered losses [23]; (16) Avoided selling defective products and (17) Demanded personal assistance from the insurance company [24]

Insurers: (1) Selected insurers with the highest liquidity and solvency and (2) Subscribed an insurance newsletter containing information on insurers' reputation and claims' payment history

Insurance: _General_: (1) Created risk analysis questionnaires; (2) Requested employees to fulfill them; (3) Screened answers for misstatements; (4) Assessed the company's insurance needs; (5) Analyzed insurers and their insurance proposals aiming to meet these needs; (6) Defined criteria for proposal selection; (7) Selected the most appropriate ones; (8) Explained to employees the most important terms and clauses of insurance contracts; (9) Hired an insurance agent to reduce outsiders' costs; _Life, Health and Dental_: (1) Balanced life and work so that employees can live longer and healthier lives; (2) Estimated the amount of life insurance required [25]; (3) Identified primary beneficiaries [26]; (4) Discussed with the employees about the coverage and exclusions of policies; (5) Incorporated benefits in employee compensation; (6) Met minimum participation requirements [27]; (7) Selected contribution patterns [28]; (8) Compared defined-contribution with defined-benefit private retirement plans [29]; _Home_: (1) Evaluated property coverage, perils insured against and exclusions; (2) Explained to the insured their duties in case a loss occurs; _Auto_: (1) Installed alarm systems inside vehicles; (2) Shifted from auto insurance policies to a package of car finder and car blocker in case of theft and car assistance in case of breakdown; (3) Gathered information on the profile of company drivers; (4) Identified the parties that are insured by the liability coverage; (5) Asked the company's drivers to take more care when they drive; (6) Explained to drivers the covered and excluded risks; (7) Forbid company's drivers to drive under the effect of alcohol; (8) Hired drivers over X years old and with no records of car accidents in the previous Y years; _Property_: (1) Passed physical inspection [30]; (2) Evaluated property risks [31]; (3) Evaluated optional coverage [32]; (4) Identified causes of loss for claims [33]; _Liability_: (1) Analyzed which liabilities and which amount should be covered by a policy [34]; (2) Evaluated employers' liability policies [35]; (3) Analyzed the covered and excluded risks [36]; (4) Decided to contract an employee liability insurance policy; (5) Concluded that coverage for liabilities within the company's premises and operations, products, contracts and contingencies was required; _Crime_: (1) Implemented a security system that reduced crime loss exposures and thus reduced the crime insurance policy premium and (2) Selected location with low crime exposure to settle down our office and factory

3.18.Quality Management

Quality Management comprises professional accomplishments related to the monitoring of quality aspects of the products and services the company makes available either to the industrial or to the consumer market or to both:

QUALITY MANAGEMENT:

Strategic management: (1) Was nominated quality manager; (2) Created the organization's policy on quality [1]; (3) Forwarded copies of the policy to stakeholders [2]; (4) Wrote up a quality manual [3]; (5) Adapted the structure of ISO9001 to our manufacturing case [4]; (6) Applied for and Received the ISO9001 certification; (7) Kept up-to-date with new and existing quality norms; (8) Defined quality objectives [5]; (9) Maintained quality-related records for X fiscal years in a place only known to in-charge employees and (10) Established a quality management program

Analysis: (1) Assessed current production performance regarding quality [6] and (2) Established numerical improvement targets [7]

Planning: *Operations*: (1) Balanced the benefits and costs of quality assurance [8]; (2) Wrote up technical procedures [9]; (3) Created processes' flowcharts [10]; (4) Developed work instructions [11]; (5) Forwarded procedures, processes' flowcharts and work instructions to involved staff; (6) Validated them; (7) Calculated the quality department budget [12]; (8) Created checklists; (9) Established quality-related key performance indicators [13]; (10) Developed the organizational chart regarding quality management [14]; (11) Produced drawings; (12) Linked procedures, processes and work instructions to standards [15]; (13) Protected customers' intellectual property used for manufacturing [16]; (14) Visited the customers to better understand their needs [17]; (15) Defined criteria for product acceptability [18]; (16) Avoided over-specification [19]; (17) Developed suppliers' self-evaluation questionnaires; *Emergencies*: (1) Analyzed the Materials Safety Data Sheet of all raw materials; (5) Assessed risks and (6) Found out potential hazards

Execution: (1) Organized activities and resources [20]; (2) Assured internal and external quality control [21]; (3) Designed X products and Y services; (4) Enabled their pricing in a competitive fashion; (5) Received customer feedback on quality of product samples [22]; (6) Gathered proofs of quality level [23]; (7) Provided technical assistance and maintenance; (8) Coordinated the R&D laboratory; (9) Examined packing; (10) Provided continual improvement of the quality management system [24]; (11) Calibrated equipment; (12) Certified X products in Y Accredited Certification Bodies; (13) Printed products' lot numbers on their packages; (14) Complied with internationally agreed safety standards; (15) Tested products and (16) Carried out field tests to evaluate product performance

Control: *Measurement*: (1) Controlled on a daily basis the quality of the company's products and services [25]; (2) Selected a method for monitoring [26]; (3) Monitored all stages of production process [27]; (4) Cut waste generation by X%; (5) Enhanced product reliability by Y%; (6) Boosted customer satisfaction by X%; (7) Reduced number of defective output by Y%; (8) Increased product mean life by X%; (9) Lowered the failure rate by Y%; (10) Improved product function and appearance; *Nonconformities*: (1) Established a complaint hotline; (2) Designed quality questionnaires [28]; (3) Interviewed stakeholders on quality issues; (4) Managed nonconforming processes [29]; (5) Took remedial actions to mitigate nonconformities [30]; (6) Investigated underlying reasons for nonconformities [31]; (7) Acted toward avoiding their recurrence [32]; (8) Kept records of corrective and preventive actions' outcomes [33]; (9) Researched on the effectiveness of actions; (10) Changed procedures as required; (11) Segregated finished products that presented poor quality [34]; *Audit*: (1) Prepared an audit plan [35]; (2) Created audit checklists; (3) Oftentimes Carried out an internal quality audit [36]; (4) Determined the compliance with ISO9001 [37]; (5) Recorded audit outcomes [38]; (6) Informed them to the Board of Directors; (7) Hired an expert to audit our main suppliers; (8) Qualified internal auditors; (9) Scheduled both internal and external audits [39]; (10) Defined audits' scopes [40] and (11) Prepared answers to typical auditor inquiries

Staff development: (1) Educated employees responsible for product quality [41]; (2) Regarding measures we monitor, Trained staff to reduce those undesirable and increase the desirable ones; (3) Participated at quality planning seminars; (4) Trained technical staff to use testing equipment; (5) Documented training sessions [42]; (6) Evaluated the effectiveness of training [43] and (7) Created a quality assurance team

3.19.Environmental Management

The professional activities regarding Environmental Management involve monitoring the relationship between the company and the natural environment, pursuing the protection of the latter:

ENVIRONMENTAL MANAGEMENT:

Strategic management: (1) Created the organization's environmental policy [1]; (2) Sent copies of the policy to stakeholders [2]; (3) Developed an environmental management system's manual [3]; (4) Applied for and Got the ISO14001 certification; (5) Kept up-to-date with new and existing environmental regulations; (6) Developed suppliers' self-evaluation questionnaires [4]; (7) Stored environment-related documents for X fiscal years in a place only accessible to designated staff; (8) Established an environmental management program [5]

Analysis: (1) Researched on the company's past environmental performance [6]; (2) Deemed noise, air, water and soil aspects of pollution [7]; (3) Developed reports of both positive and negative impacts of the company's operations, products and sites on the natural environment and its living species; (4) Assessed current environmental performance [8]; (5) Established numerical improvement goals; (6) Ranked impacts in order of priority to deal with [9]; (7) Assessed environmental impacts whenever a process change took place [10]

Planning: *Operations*: (1) Created a procedure to analyze environmental impacts in order to unveil the relative importance of multiple points of view [11]; (2) Listed environmental effects under regular operation conditions [12]; (3) Applied and Got authorization from the government to store and sell chemicals; (4) Designated activities to areas of our facility; *Emergencies*: (1) Trained staff on what to do in case of a myriad of different emergency situations [13]; (2) Paid Attention in order to avoid accidental emissions to atmosphere and accidental discharges to water and soil [14]; (3) Evaluated the hazard from accidental releases caused to ecosystems [15]; (4) Studied the Materials Safety Data Sheet of all raw materials

Execution: (1) Allocated the human, technical, and financial resources necessary to meet the factory's environmental goals [16]; (2) Recycled water used in one production process to be utilized in another one [17]; (3) Reused water for cleaning the floor [18]; (4) Set energy-saving devices at our factory and office [19]; (5) Avoided, as long as possible, land contamination and releases to the atmosphere within production sites; (6) Bought a piece of land to preserve wildlife habitats; (7) Designed products and services to minimize their negative environmental impact from production to disposal [20]; (8) Recycled solid wastes; (9) Controlled hazardous raw materials; (10) Struggled for sustainable development [21]; (11) Coordinated the R&D laboratory; (12) Organized the handling and storage of raw materials; (13) Organized daily operational activities; (14) Responded to changing environmental requirements [22]; (15) Minimized the impact of our transport operations [23]; (16) Besides a cost-benefit analysis, Deemed the environmental impacts of our suppliers [24]; (17) Draw a scratch of the plant showing its discharges points and Created a spreadsheet with annual measured discharges [25]; (18) Selected weighing factors for each environmental effect and Calculated scores [26] and (19) Carried out continual improvement of the environmental management system [27]

Control: *Measurement*: (1) Monitored all the measured variables [28]; (2) Established time horizons for measures; (3) Cut waste generation by X%; (4) Decreased the release of pollutant agents into the natural environment by Y%; (5) Reduced the production of wastewater by X%; (6) Slashed CO_2 emissions by Y%; (7) Cut energy utilization by X%; (8) Decreased utilized water by Y%; (9) Reduced consumption of fuel by X%; (10) Slashed lead emissions by Y%; (11) Cut emission of nitrogen oxides by X%; (12) Reduced ozone-depleting substances' consumption by Y%; (13) Followed up the waste per weight and number of pieces of each product we manufacture; *Nonconformities*: (1) Identified and Registered all meaningful environmental accidents [29]; (2) Took corrective actions to mitigate their environmental impacts [30]; (3) Investigated underlying reasons for nonconformities [31]; (4) Acted toward avoiding their recurrence [32]; (5) Kept records of corrective and preventive actions' outcomes [33]; (6) Researched on the effectiveness of actions [34]; (7) Changed procedures as required; *Audit*: (1) Created audit checklists [35]; (2) Periodically Carried out an internal environmental audit [36]; (3) Determined the compliance with ISO14001 [37]; (4) Recorded audit outcomes [38] and (5) Informed them to the Board of Directors [39]

Education: (1) Regarding measures we monitor, Trained staff to reduce those undesirable and increase the desirable ones [40]; (2) Participated at environmental planning seminars; (3) Documented training sessions [41]; (4) Evaluated the effectiveness of training [42]; (5) Created awareness of the natural environment inside the company and in its neighborhood; (6) Established partnerships with research institutes and (7) Shared know-how on environmental issues with suppliers and customers

Communication: (1) Communicated commitment to environmental protection [43]; (2) Dealt with legal issues in the interface between the environment and our organization activities, products and services [44]; (3) Informed stakeholders on the company's environmental performance [45]; (4) Published environmental reports and Forwarded them company-wide [46] and (5) Surveyed public opinion about our factory's environmental programs

3.20.Social Responsibility

Social Responsibility comprises professional activities carried out by a company, but whose purpose is to do good things for both the company and the society in general:

SOCIAL RESPONSIBILITY:

Strategy: Aligned the objectives of the Social Responsibility department with the Millennium Development Goals [1] created by the United Nations (UN)

<u>Millennium Development Goals</u>: (2001-2015) *Eradicate extreme poverty and hunger* [2]: (1) Donated resources for hunger-fighting NGOs; (2) Placed the company's lowest salary above the minimum salary stipulated by the country's government; *Reach universal primary education* [3]: (1) During the admission exam, Asked, among other questions, some covering the elementary school program, and for those that didn't succeed in replying, Taught how to solve them; *Promote equality between genders and Empower women* [4]: (1) Hired approximately the same number of male and female employees; (2) Kept this same equilibrium in the Board composition; *Reduce children mortality* [5]: (1) Donated either groceries or disposable diapers to female employees belonging to disadvantaged economic classes when they became mothers; *Improve health of pregnant women* [6]: (1) Allowed pregnant women to be absent from work even without presenting a medical certificate when they informed they stayed resting at home as a result of pregnancy illness; *Combat HIV/AIDS, malaria and other diseases* [7]: (1) Eliminated all objects that could store standing still water to prevent egg deposition of the mosquitoes that transmit diseases such as 'dengue'; *Assure the environmental sustainability* [8]: (1) Implemented photovoltaic cells to seize solar energy in X properties of the company (located in Y cities) and *Global*

partnership for the development [9]: (1) Followed up news at UN website, as well as global initiatives in terms of the millennium development goals, in order to select those that could well be applied by our company

Corporate Social Initiatives: (1) Chose initiatives that echo business goals [10]; (2) Improved world living conditions and simultaneously boosted sales [11]; (3) Supported a cause that relates closely to our corporate brand [12]; (4) Developed environmentally friendly products [13]; (5) Strengthened our organization's image [14]; (6) Planned a different type of initiative for each year's campaign in order to be innovative; (7) Discussed internally about the best way to allocate resources, people, time, messages and events; (8) Attracted and Retained highly-motivated employees that are sensitive to the causes the company focuses on [15]; (9) Decreased operating costs [16]; (10) Decreased publicity budgets [17]; (11) Reduced wastes [18]; (12) Reused materials [19]; (13) Recycled [20]; (14) Saved water and electricity [21]; (15) Improved the way investors and financial analysts look at our organization [22]; (16) Accessed loans more easily [23]; (17) Selected social issues that our competitors are not caring about [24]; (18) Despite the due social involvement, Remained focused on the core business; (19) Drew attention from the most enthusiastic public audience about the initiative [25]; (20) Determined the socio-demographic characteristics of this target audience [26]; (21) Created leaflets to advertise the initiative and invite the right people to take part at it; (22) Calculated the budget of the initiative [27]; (23) Collected money from supporters [28]; (24)

Invited celebrities to provide a supporting speech; (25) Encouraged participants to give a helping hand to the cause [29]; (26) Led a behavior change toward the cause [30]; (27) Researched about the initiative effectiveness after it took place [31]; (28) Took corrective action in the following years in order to avoid perceived mistakes in earlier campaigns [32] and (29) Provided feedback to society with improved facts & figures resulting from the initiative, as long as informing our long-term commitment to the targeted social cause [33]

3.21.Real Estate

Real Estate involves professional activities such as managing land properties so that they maximize the owners' profits:

REAL ESTATE:

Negotiation: *Planning*: (1) Used information about a transaction to shape upcoming transactions [1]; *Sales*: (1) Created properties' sales policies; (2) Showed properties to potential clients; (3) Screened the buyer for uniqueness that would drive profit up [2]; (4) Kept price to the buyer up [3]; (5) Avoid selling for less than market value [4]; (6) Segmented our clientele in the space market according to purpose and ownership [5]; (7) Used credit management information to reduce the default risk; (8) Carried out selling transactions; *Acquisitions*: (1) Wrote up properties' purchases policies; (2) Visited target properties; (3) Drove seller's price down [6]; (4) Avoided paying more than the market value [7]; (5) Selected the best locations for our offices and factories; (6) Executed acquisition transactions; *Rentals*: (1) Developed properties' leasing policies; (2) Rented properties to tenants willing to pay higher rent [8]; (3) Built expected bid-rent functions for several land uses [9] and Made the highest and best use of land [10]; (4) Improved buildings to persuade current tenants to stay longer; (5) Improved properties to talk potential tenants into signing long-term rental contracts; (6) Calculated the expected vacancy rates; (7) Determined rent values and Got agreement from the tenant; (8) Determined effective rents [11]; (9) Evaluated the tradeoff between releasing costs and the value of flexibility to enhance lease terms [12]; (10) Booked more space to tenants able to increase profits of other commercial tenants [13]; (11) Kept secret the actual rent and Unveiled publicly a higher rent than the accrued one [14]; (12) Maximized building value at usual vacancy rates of X% and (13) Executed leasing transactions

Valuation: (1) Calculated approximately how much each asset is worth [15]; (2) Decided which properties or projects to invest in; (3) Estimated the risk in the future level of expected rents; (4) Estimated the depreciation of structures built in our properties; (5) Followed up inflation trends; (6) Built a spreadsheet plotting income from properties versus several time horizons [16] and (7) Projected future selling prices of properties [17];

Investments: _Domestic_: (1) Created investment policies; (2) Kept up-to-date with real estate market news; (3) Evaluated the company owners' profiles as investors; (4) Estimated the opportunity cost of capital [18]; (5) Diversified investments [19] to mitigate risks; (6) Met a target long-term overall expected total return of X% per year for a collection of investment funds; (7) Invested in funds seeming to be underpriced; (8) Interrupted investments in funds apparently overpriced; (8) Created a decision tree with feasible outcomes for real estate investment decisions; (9) Analyzed issues of control and governance before investing; (10) Calculated expected returns; (11) Evaluated the risk of a myriad of commercial properties; (12) Used law-abiding tax shields [20]; _International_: (1) Assessed costs and risks [21] and Entered global real estate markets; (2) Defined own optimal international investment strategies [22]; (3) Managed currency risks [23]; (4) Determined entry timing and (5) Determined optimal resource allocation among countries or territories [24]

Real options: (1) Exercised options; (2) Analyzed options; (3) Waited net present value of options to be positively high enough to select the best courses of action [25]; (4) Selected construction timing with maximum net present value [26]; (5) Completed fully operational revenue-generating buildings; (6) Calculated expected return [27]; (7) Calculated the investment return risk ratio [28]; (8) Analyzed the tradeoff between time and risk [29]; (9) Plotted the valuation probabilities [30] for optimistic, expected and pessimistic scenarios and (10) Avoided overbuilding

Development projects: (1) Carried out a financial, market and competitive analysis [31]; (2) Conducted a physical and design analysis [32]; (3) Assessed political and legal implications [33]; (4) Plotted time, cumulative investment and risk level of real estate development projects [34]; (5) Determined the highest and best use of sites [35]; (6) Ordered priorities in investment payback [36]; (7) Estimated land and construction costs [37]; (8) Included contingency amounts for unexpected costs [38]; (9) Reviewed construction budgets; (10) Calculated the lowest rent per square meter of built structure for which rental would be financially feasible [39]; (11) Determined time required to ready buildings for use [40]; (12) Calculated opportunity costs of capital [41]; (13) Ranked projects [42]; (14) Computed the development value at each phase of the project [43]; (15) Examined multi-phase developments [44]; (16) Divided projects into steps [45] and (17) Analyzed the feasibility of building several types of development on a piece of land [46]

3.22. Example of a one-page CV

Till now hundreds of examples of winning professional accomplishments have been presented, those that make up a detailed CV. Inside the company's computer, the candidate can store information on these accomplishments in digital files. However, should the objective of the candidate be to synthesize information and to present a one-page CV, only his or her most important professional accomplishments ought to be written. Hereunder follows one example:

BUSINESS EXPERIENCE

Beginning   Company, City, Country

End   *Job Position*

1. Corporate Governance: Familiar with the Sarbanes-Oxley Act from 2002

2. Strategy: Selected a competitive strategy and Planned actions for potentially likely situations

3. Administration: Defined the organization chart, Opened X branch offices, Controlled corporate results

4. Organizational Culture: Chose the key performance indicator to pay primary attention, Wrote stories to tell to newcomers, Provided to the company its own cultural profile

5. Law: Gathered evidence, Assisted in writing up civil processes, Revised contract clauses

6. <u>Operations</u>: Maximized the use of operational bottlenecks, Implemented approaches to enhance operational efficiency and effectiveness

7. <u>Negotiation</u>: Planned and Conducted negotiations, Evaluated outcomes and Mitigated imperfections

8. <u>Marketing</u>: Updated mix, Generated $ X million of revenue (Y orders – X clients), Created Y brands

9. <u>Foreign Trade</u>: Collected data on the global market, Issued documents & Followed shipments, Calculated costs & selling prices, Developed network of exporters, importers & shipping agents

10. <u>Supply Management</u>: Reduced $ X thousand in costs, Brought Y suppliers & X products

11. <u>Human Resources</u>: Announced vacancies, Interviewed, Selected, Evaluated operational metrics, Trained, Created career center, Communicated performance, Increased retention

12. <u>Organizational Behavior</u>: Honed own leadership skills, Supervised staff

13. <u>Accounting</u>: Controlled financial ratios and Defined policies for future actions through benchmarking

14. <u>Credit Management</u>: Controlled creditworthiness and cash collection reports, Calculated measures of credit and solvency

15. Finance: Evaluated and Applied in investment funds, Evaluated how much the company is worth

16. Economics: Reduced unemployment by hiring employees when many companies were downsizing

17. Insurance: As an insurance broker, Managed insurable risks in the fields of Auto, Life and Home

18. Quality & Environmental Management: Fulfilled supplier self-evaluation questionnaires, Translated X Material Safety Data Sheets

19. Social Responsibility: Contributed to the UN Millennium Development Goals (2000-2015)

20. Real Estate: Showed properties in order to sell, Visited properties in order to purchase

3.23. Final considerations on business experience

Firstly, some topics appear more than once (such as Strategy, Human Resources and Organizational Culture) because some professionals have only one of the other subjects treated in the book and wish to present a small participation in these subjects.

Secondly, should the organization of the executive be a private company, such as a limited liability company, he or she can still read and become familiar with the law that underpins the corporate governance of publicly held companies, this document can be easily downloaded for free on the internet, and he or she can put on the CV the following:

Corporate Governance: (1) Familiar with the Sarbannes-Oxley Act from 2002

This simple phrase can be useful to help the candidate to be invited for a job interview in case he or she intends to work for a publicly held company.

Yet should the company of the professional not yet operate in the international marketplace, he or she can read the legislation concerning what is required to be able to practice foreign trade, and write:

Foreign Trade: (1) Familiar with the procedure to become an importer/exporter

And if the company of the professional happens to get an authorization to operate in the foreign marketplace, he or she will be able to state:

Foreign Trade: (1) Carried out the insertion of the company in the foreign marketplace as an importer or exporter or both

Furthermore, when the professional accomplishment states what the company should do, the reader must pay attention to justify this decision, in this way the accomplishment is not absolute but circumstantial; denying or simply modifying the course of action to be taken may be more convenient, provided there is a plausible underlying reason. For instance, should a recruiter lack time in the candidates' selection process, this Human Resources professional can mention in the CV:

Human Resources: (1) Denied the conduction of a $360°$ analysis of candidates and Carried out a fast selection process

Should for certain job positions be important a deep analysis of the candidates' professional profile, this same Human Resources Manager will be able to mention the opposite in his or her own CV:

<u>Human Resources</u>: (1) Carried out a 360° analysis of candidates for key positions

Finally, not all the companies do possess quality and environmental management systems. But many of them deal with those who have these systems. Then the following phrase can be put in the CV:

<u>Quality Management and Environmental Management</u>: (1) Fulfilled supplier self-evaluation questionnaires sent by customers certified by the ISO9001 and ISO14001 norms

Following the same kind of reasoning presented till here throughout this section of the chapter, other modifications and insertions can take place to adapt the teachings of the book to the readers' reality.

Chapter 4 – Information Technology Experience

The information technology experience comprises hardware mastery and software mastery.

4.1.Hardware mastery

Regarding hardware, the minimum knowledge that the business professional must possess is the one that enables the use of hardware equipment in a safe and effective manner. For this minimum knowledge it would seem that there are neither standardized international exams nor certificates. A little bit wider knowledge that may interest some business professionals consists of knowing how to distinguish hardware equipment from several manufacturers, as well as knowing the advantages and disadvantages of each one. It would seem that some of the main manufacturers of hardware throughout the world [1] are Lenovo [2], Hewlett Packard [3], Dell [4], Acer [5] and Apple [6]. Some of the main hardware manufacturers worldwide offer standardized exams and certificates for the knowledge of their own hardware equipment at the sales level, as follows:

Lenovo

Certifications: Lenovo Certified Enterprise Server Technical Sales Professional and Lenovo Certified Enterprise Server Sales Professional

Useful link:

http://www.lenovopartnernetwork.com/lcp-workpage

Hewlett Packard

Certifications: HPE Sales Certified – Enterprise Solutions and HPE Sales Certified SMB Solutions and Services

Useful link:

http://certification-learning.hpe.com/tr/certifications

Yet the technical knowledge of how to fix hardware equipment is not required for a business professional in general, but should the candidate present interest in this field, there are also standardized examinations and certifications.

4.2.Software mastery

Regarding software, the minimum knowledge that the business professional must possess is the mastery of application programs that enable building texts, spreadsheets, charts and presenting slides, besides the mastery of a multifunctional corporate program, that is, one that issues invoices, coordinates credit collection, presents the history of the relationship with clients and suppliers, generates inventory lists, among other functions. A wider knowledge that may interest some business professionals consists of knowing details of application programs and getting certifications that attest this knowledge. Microsoft [1] offers standardized exams for the knowledge of its application programs, as follows:

Exam 418 – Microsoft Office Word 2013 [2]

Exam 419 – Microsoft SharePoint 2013 [3]

Exam 420 – Microsoft Office Excel 2013 [4]

Exam 421 – Microsoft Office OneNote 2013 [5]

Exam 422 – Microsoft Office PowerPoint 2013 [6]

Exam 423 – Microsoft Office Outlook 2013 [7]

Exam 424 – Microsoft Office Access 2013 [8]

Exams 425 e 426 –Microsoft Office Word 2013 Expert [9]

Exams 427 e 428 – Microsoft Office Excel 2013 Expert [10]

As soon as new versions of these application programs become available, new examinations will pop up. According to some criteria, the following certifications are issued for those who succeed in the exams above:

Microsoft Office Specialist [11]

Microsoft Office Specialist Expert [12]

Microsoft Office Specialist Master [13]

Useful link: https://www.microsoft.com/pt-br/learning/certification-overview.aspx

4.3.Example of a detailed CV

INFORMATION TECHNOLOGY EXPERIENCE

Hardware: *Lenovo*: Lenovo Certified Enterprise Server Technical Sales Professional and Lenovo Certified Enterprise Server Sales Professional; *Hewlett Packard*: HPE Sales Certified – Enterprise Solutions and HPE Sales Certified SMB Solutions and Services; Software: *Microsoft*: Microsoft Office Specialist; Microsoft Office Specialist Expert and Microsoft Office Specialist Master

4.4. Example of a one-page CV

INFORMATION TECHNOLOGY EXPERIENCE

<u>Hardware</u>: Received X certifications issued by the main computer manufacturers worldwide; <u>Software</u>: Approved in Y Microsoft exams, having received X certifications

4.5. Final considerations on information technology experience

Regarding the mastery of hardware, the professionals that do possess certificates of hardware manufacturers don't need to cite where they learned, leaving this information to be told during the job interview. It is enough to state in the CV the name of the certificate. Yet who doesn't possess any certificate can put in the CV basic information about hardware studies, that is, the school name (or self-study), location, name of the courses he or she attended and their total duration, as follows:

<u>Hardware</u>: *Lenovo, Hewlett Packard, Dell, Acer & Apple*: School "Name" (country), Basic, Intermediate and Advanced courses (total duration Y hours distributed in X years – Beginning/End)

Regarding the mastery of software, the professionals that do possess Microsoft certificates don't need to cite where they learned, leaving this information to be told during the job interview. It is enough to state in the CV the name of the certificate. Yet who doesn't possess any certificate can put in the CV basic information about software studies, that is, the school name (or self-study), location, name of the courses he or she attended and their total duration, as follows:

Software: *Microsoft Word, Excel, PowerPoint, Access, Outlook, OneNote, Sharepoint*: School "Name" (country), Basic, Intermediate and Advanced courses (total duration Y hours distributed in X years – Beginning/End)

Chapter 5 – International Experience

The international experience entails the mastery of foreign languages and the relationship with foreign countries.

5.1.Mastery of foreign languages

The mastery of foreign languages is demonstrated through the results of a test created and corrected by an international examination body and administered at examination centers located in several countries. For each language there is one or more examination boards, which issue a certificate attesting that the candidate possesses a certain level of mastery in a foreign language, irrespective of the place and method of learning. The levels of mastery are: A1 (lower basic), A2 (higher basic), B1 (lower intermediate), B2 (higher intermediate), C1 (lower advanced) e C2 (higher advanced). This system of levels was created by Europe several years ago and enabled to standardize the results because it applies to all the languages. For further information on this system, also called Common European Framework Reference for Languages (CEFR), visit www.coe.int, where you will find descriptions of what the speaker can do in each level, in terms of written comprehension and expression and about oral comprehension and expression.

Hereunder are listed some of the main examination boards worldwide for foreign languages:

Cambridge University (General, Business, Legal and Financial English)

Names of the exams: KET, PET, FCE, CAE, CPE, BEC P, BEC V, BEC H, ILEC, ICFE

Useful link: www.cambridgeenglish.org/

Trinity College London (General, Oral and Business English)

Names of the exams: ISE, GESE, SEW

Useful link:

http://www.trinitycollege.com/site/?id=263

Confucius Institute (General, Oral and Business Chinese)

Names of the exams: HSK, HSKK, BCT

Useful links: http://english.hanban.org/

http://www.chinaeducenter.com/en/

http://www.chinesetest.cn/index.do

Instituto Cervantes (General Spanish)

Names of the exams: DELE

Useful link: http://diplomas.cervantes.es/

Camara de Madrid (Business, Health Sciences and Tourism Spanish)

Exams' initials: CBEN, CSEN, DEN, CBECS, CSECS, CBET, CSET

Useful link:

http://www.camaramadrid.es/asp/cursos/buscador2.asp

Centre International d'Etudes Pedagogiques (General French)
Names of the exams: DELF, DALF
Useful link: www.ciep.fr

Chambre de Commerce et d'Industrie de Paris (General, Business, Legal, Technical and Scientific, Medical, Tourism, Diplomacy and International Relations, Fashion and Secretariat French)
Exams' initials: DFP
Useful link: www.francais.cci-paris-idf.fr

Instituto Nacional de Estudos e Pesquisas Educacionais Anisio Teixeira (General Portuguese)
Names of the exams: CELPE-BRAS
Useful link: http://portal.inep.gov.br/celpebras/

Centro de Avaliacao de Portugues Lingua Estrangeira (General Portuguese)
Names of the exams: ACESSO, CIPLE, DEPLE, DIPLE, DAPLE, DUPLE
Useful link: http://caple.letras.ulisboa.pt/

Universita per Stranieri di Perugia (General and Commercial Italian)

Names of the exams: CELI, CIC

Useful link: www.cvcl.it

Universita per Stranieri di Siena (General Italian)

Names of the exams: CILS

Useful link: www.unistrasi.it

Goethe Institut (General and Business German)

Exams' initials: Goethe-Zertifikat, BULATS Deutsch

Useful link:

https://www.goethe.de/de/spr/kup/prf/prf.html

Japan Foundation & Japan Educational Exchanges and Services (General Japanese)

Names of the exams: JLPT

Useful link:http://www.jlpt.jp/e/

Russian Ministry of Education and Science (General Russian)

Names of the exams: TORFL

Useful link: http://www.torfl.org/en

National Institute for International Education (General Korean)

Names of exams: TOPIK

Useful Links:

http://www.niied.go.kr/eng/contents.do?contentsNo=88&menuNo=359

http://www.topik.go.kr/usr/cmm/subLocation.do?menuSeq=2210101

Note: In the list above, some graphic signals pertaining to French, Italian, Portuguese and Spanish languages have been omitted.

5.2.Relationship with foreign countries

The relationship with foreign countries manifests itself by means of the penetration of the company in the international market, what can occur through the establishment of overseas branch offices (manufacturing or distributing units), or even via phone or email and more importantly personally through either foreign trips or reception of foreign employees in the candidates' country. Study and Tourism stays abroad also enrich the CV.

5.3. Example of a detailed CV

In order to present the mastery of foreign languages in a detailed CV, one should build a table with all the certificates, indicating their level and examination board, and even highlighting in bold letters the certificates with the highest level attained in each language. In order to summarize information for the recruiter, a chart or table classifying certificates by level, language and subject may be presented. In order to present the relationship with foreign countries, the basic information is the names of the countries and the total length of stay, which can be stated through a table.

INTERNATIONAL EXPERIENCE

Communication Skills:

Examination Board	N	Certificate Name	Level
University of Cambridge	1	Key English Test	A2
	2	Preliminary English Test	B1
	3	First Certificate in English	B2
	4	Certificate in Advanced English	C1
	5	**Certificate of Proficiency in English**	**C2**
	6	Business English Certificate –	B1

		Preliminary Level	
	7	Business English Certificate – Vantage Level	B2
	8	Business English Certificate – Higher Level	C1
	9	International Legal English Certificate	C1
	10	International Certificate in Financial English	C1
Centre International d'Etudes Pedagogiques	11	Diplome d'Etudes en Langue Francaise – Niveau A1	A1
	12	Diplome d'Etudes en Langue Francaise – Niveau A2	A2
	13	Diplome d'Etudes en Langue Francaise – Niveau B1	B1
	14	Diplome d'Etudes en Langue Francaise – Niveau B2	B2
	15	Diplome Approfondi en Langue Francaise – Niveau C1	C1
	16	**Diplome Approfondi en Langue Francaise – Niveau C2**	**C2**
Chambre de Commerce et	17	Diplome de Francais des Professions – Affaires – B2	B2

d'Industrie de Paris	18	Diplome de Francais des Professions – Affaires – C1	C1
	19	**Diplome de Francais des Professions – Affaires – C2**	**C2**
	20	Diplome de Francais des Professions – Juridique	B2
	21	Diplome de Francais des Professions Scientifique&Technique	B1
Universita per Stranieri di Perugia	22	Certificato di Conoscenza della Lingua Italiana – Impatto	A1
	23	Certificato di Conoscenza della Lingua Italiana – Livello 1	A2
	24	Certificato di Conoscenza della Lingua Italiana – Livello 2	B1
	25	Certificato di Conoscenza della Lingua Italiana – Livello 3	B2
	26	Certificato di Conoscenza della Lingua Italiana – Livello 4	C1
	27	**Certificato di Conoscenza della Lingua Italiana – Livello 5**	**C2**
	28	Certificato di Italiano Commerciale – Livello Intermedio	B1

	29	Certificato di Italiano Commerciale – Livello Avanzato	C1
Instituto Cervantes	30	Diploma de Espanol Lengua Extranjera – Nivel A1	A1
	31	Diploma de Espanol Lengua Extranjera – Nivel A2	A2
	32	Diploma de Espanol Lengua Extranjera – Nivel Inicial	B1
	33	Diploma de Espanol Lengua Extranjera – Nivel Intermedio	B2
	34	Diploma de Espanol Lengua Extranjera – Nivel C1	C1
	35	**Diploma de Espanol Lengua Extranjera – Nivel Superior**	**C2**
Camara de Madrid	36	Certificado Basico de Espanol de los Negocios	B2
	37	Certificado Superior de Espanol de los Negocios	C1
	38	**Diploma de Espanol de los Negocios**	**C2**

Note: In the table above, some graphic signals pertaining to French, Italian and Spanish languages have been omitted.

Summary of Language Certificates:

Language	A1	A2	B1	B2	C1	C2	Total
English	-	1	2	2	4	1	10
French	1	1	2	3	2	2	11
Italian	1	1	2	1	2	1	8
Spanish	1	1	1	2	2	2	9
Total	3	4	7	8	10	6	38

Language	English	French	Italian	Spanish	Total
General	5	6	6	6	23
Business	3	3	2	3	11
Legal	1	1	-	-	2
Financial	1	-	-	-	1
Technical	-	1	-	-	1
Total	10	11	8	9	38

Internationalism:

N	Country	Length of stay	N	Country	Length of stay
1	USA	3 months	11	France	20 days
2	Canada	15 days	12	Italy	7 days
3	Mexico	7 days	13	Germany	21 days
4	Argentina	1 month	14	S. Africa	7 days
5	Paraguay	15 days	15	Egypt	10 days
6	Uruguay	5 days	16	China	1 month
7	Aruba	7 days	17	Japan	18 days
8	Curacao	1 day	18	S.Korea	6 days
9	Portugal	6 days	19	Russia	2 days
10	Spain	16 days	20	Australia	9 days

5.4.Example of a one-page CV

In order to present the mastery of foreign languages in a one-page CV, the level of mastery should be written beside the name of each language, then the number of certificates should be stated. In order to present the relationship with foreign countries, it is enough to cite the number of countries. If the candidate would like to, he or she can add the number of visited cities.

INTERNATIONAL EXPERIENCE

Language Levels: English X, Chinese Y, Spanish X, French Y, Portuguese X, Italian Y, German X, Japanese Y, Russian X, Korean Y; Communication Skills: Obtained Y foreign language certificates issued by the main examination boards worldwide; Internationalism: Traveled through X countries located in America, Europe, Asia, Africa and Oceania (Y cities), Having spent over X days abroad

5.5.Final considerations on international experience

Regarding the mastery of foreign languages, the professionals that do possess international certificates issued by examination boards do not need to cite where they learned, leaving this information to be told during the job interview. It is enough to state on the CV the language level that the certificate attests. Yet those who do not possess any certificate may put on the CV that the informed level of mastery results from self-evaluation. Should this be the case, it is convenient to cite basic information about language studies, such as the school name (or self-study), location, name of the courses carried out and their total duration, as follows:

Language Levels (Self-evaluation): *English X*: School "Name" (country), Basic, Intermediate and Advanced courses (total duration Y hours distributed in X years – Beginning/End); *Spanish Y*: School "Name" (country), Basic and Intermediate courses (total duration X hours distributed in Y months – Beginning/End)

Regarding the relationship with foreign countries, the professionals that have traveled extensively need only cite the names of the countries and the length of stay in each of them, leaving the information on the activities developed there to be told during the interview. Yet those who has not traveled extensively, may add information such as the year when they traveled, trip purpose, activities developed there, names of visited companies and type of relationship with the traveler's company (plant, client, supplier, among others), as follows:

Internationalism: *United States (city)*: 5 Trips of 2 weeks each to visit key client, do follow-up and negotiate supply terms (years); *Japan (city)*: 2 Trips of 1 month each for Sales and motivation workshops, gathering managers from all branch offices worldwide (years), comprising visits to plants where our equipment is used (name of cities and companies)

References in sectional order

Section 3.1

[1] based on United States Securities and Exchange Commission (2016) Sarbanes Oxley Act 2002 https://www.sec.gov/about/laws/soa2002.pdf (accessed on June 9th, 2016)

From [2] to [38] based on Larcker, D. & Tayan, B. (2011) Corporate Governance Matters – A closer look at organizational choices and their consequences, FT Press (Pearson Education), New Jersey, United States, 480 pages, ISBN-13: 978-0-13-351850-4

[2]: 77; [3]: 72; [4]: 72; [5]: 72; [6]: 72; [7]: 72; [8]: 72; [9]: 72; [10]: 72; [11]: 73; [12]: 73; [13]: 73; [14]: 204; [15]: 73; [16]: 216; [17]: 208; [18]: 191; [19]: 189-190; [20]: 190; [21]: 191; [22]: 190; [23]: 191; [24]: 193; [25]: 194; [26]: 287; [27]: 310; [28]: 363; [29]: 362; [30]: 365; [31]: 367; [32]: 365; [33]: 373; [34]: 370; [35]: 373; [36]: 397; [37]: 401 and [38]: 433

Section 3.2

From [1] to [54] based on Porter, M.E. (1998) Competitive strategy: techniques for analyzing industries and competitors: with a new introduction, The Free Press (Simon & Schuster), New York, United States, 396 pages, ISBN-13: 978-0-684-84148-9

[1]: xxvii; [2]: 35; [3]: 35; [4]: 34; [5]: 324; [6]: 275; [7]: 4; [8]: 3; [9]: 158-161; [10]: 220; [11]: 71; [12]: 50&54; [13]: 51&54; [14]: 103; [15]: 52; [16]: 57-58; [17]: 68; [18]: 7; [19]: 10; [20]: 10; [21]: 9; [22]: 10; [23]: 18; [24]: 23; [25]: 24; [26]: 113; [27]: 120; [28]: 118; [29]: 110; [30]: 110; [31]: 121; [32]: 111; [33]: 115; [34]: 117; [35]: 119; [36]: 120; [37]: 121; [38]: 123; [39]: 124; [40]: 123; [41]: 123; [42]: 124; [43]: 88; [44]: 89; [45]: 90; [46]: 101; [47]: 93; [48]: 95; [49]: 102; [50]: 97; [51]: 98; [52]: 106; [53]: 106 and [54]: 86-87

Section 3.3

From [1] to [96] based on Daft, R. L. & Marcic, D. (2015) Understanding Management, 9th Edition, Cengage Learning, Stamford, United States, 720 pages, ISBN-13: 978-1-285-42123-0

[1]: 77; [2]: 78; [3]: 79; [4]: 87; [5]: 87; [6]: 182; [7]: 194; [8]: 189; [9]: 193; [10]: 194; [11]: 204; [12]: 199; [13]: 199; [14]: 188; [15]: 188; [16]: 182; [17]: 189; [18]: 188; [19]: 188; [20]: 164; [21]: 164; [22]: 164; [23]: 164; [24]: 164; [25]: 165; [26]: 166; [27]: 264; [28]: 287; [29]: 271; [30]: 292; [31]: 266; [32]: 290; [33]: 377; [34]: 355; [35]: 377; [36]: 361; [37]: 526; [38]: 532; [39]: 518; [40]: 376&508; [41]: 376; [42]: 531; [43]: 373; [44]: 376; [45]: 551; [46]: 566; [47]: 556; [48]: 559-560; [49]: 560; [50]: 560; [51]: 567; [52]: 595; [53]: 596; [54]: 596; [55]: 598; [56]: 598; [57]: 598; [58]: 600-601; [59]: 601; [60]: 609; [61]: 608; [62]: 100; [63]: 103; [64]: 107; [65]: 109; [66]: 108; [67]: 111-112; [68]: 319; [69]: 315; [70]: 327; [71]: 313; [72]: 632; [73]: 633; [74]: 633; [75]: 634-635; [76]: 637-638; [77]: 641; [78]: 647; [79]: 649; [80]: 43; [81]: 222; [82]: 222; [83]: 229; [84]: 229; [85]: 229; [86]: 229; [87]: 236; [88]: 237; [89]: 238; [90]: 239; [91]: 419; [92]: 420; [93]: 432; [94]: 436; [95]: 443-444 and [96]: 447

Section 3.4.

From [1] to [70] based on Schein, E. H. (2010) Organizational Culture and Leadership, 4th Edition, Jossey-Bass (John Wiley & Sons), San Francisco, United States, 436 pages, ISBN-13: 978-0-470-19060-9

[1]: 302; [2]: 202; [3]: 84; [4]: 74; [5]: 88; [6]: 94; [7]: 98; [8]: 94; [9]: 94; [10]: 109; [11]: 111; [12]: 126; [13]: 130; [14]: 131; [15]: 140; [16]: 150; [17]: 150; [18]: 153; [19]: 219; [20]: 235; [21]: 226; [22]: 237; [23]: 240; [24]: 243; [25]: 249; [26]: 178&315; [27]: 179; [28]: 161; [29]: 178; [30]: 186; [31]: 377; [32]: 379; [33]: 318; [34]: 171; [35]: 277; [36]: 311; [37]: 279; [38]: 280; [39]: 291; [40]: 311; [41]: 294; [42]: 299; [43]: 312; [44]: 300; [45]: 303; [46]: 306; [47]: 309; [48]: 311; [49]: 366; [50]: 366; [51]: 367; [52]: 367; [53]: 369; [54]: 374; [55]: 374; [56]: 376; [57]: 376-377; [58]: 383; [59]: 379; [60]: 379; [61]: 379; [62]: 380; [63]: 386; [64]: 386; [65]: 387; [66]: 388; [67]: 388; [68]: 393; [69]: 394 and [70]: 398

Section 3.5

From [1] to [4] based on Fuhrer, M. C. A. & Fuhrer, M. R. E. (2002) Resumo de Direito Tributario, 10th edition, Volume 8, Colecao Resumos, Malheiros Editores, Sao Paulo, Brazil, 132 pages, ISBN-10: 85-7420-343-2
[1]: 50; [2]: 52&58&70; [3]: 67 and [4]: 67

From [5] to [16] based on Fuhrer, M. C. A. & Fuhrer, M. R. E. (2002) Resumo de Direito do Trabalho, 8th edition, Volume 9, Colecao Resumos, Malheiros Editores, Sao Paulo, Brazil, 191 pages, ISBN-10: 85-7420-344-0

[5]: 26; [6]: 28; [7]: 44; [8]: 47&57; [9]: 64; [10]: 68; [11]: 70; [12]: 86; [13]: 89; [14]: 101-102; [15]: 135 and [16]: 170

From [17] to [19] based on International Labor Organization (2015) ILO Declaration on fundamental principles and rights at work; http://www.ilo.org (accessed on December 12th, 2015)

[20] based on Fuhrer, M. C. A. (2002) Resumo de Processo Civil, 24th edition, Volume 4, Colecao Resumos, Malheiros Editores, Sao Paulo, Brazil, 160 pages, ISBN-10: 85-7420-339-4
[20]: 24

[21] based on Fuhrer, M. C. A. (2002) Resumo de Direito Civil, 26th edition, Volume 3, Colecao Resumos, Malheiros Editores, Sao Paulo, Brazil, 155 pages, ISBN-10: 85-7420-338-6
[21]: 87

[22] based on Fuhrer, M. C. A. (2002) Resumo de Direito Comercial, 28th edition, Volume 1, Colecao Resumos, Malheiros Editores, Sao Paulo, Brazil, 144 pages, ISBN-10: 85-7420-336-X
[22]: 26

Section 3.6

From [1] to [102] based on Stevenson, W. J. (2015) Operations Management, 12 Edition, McGraw-Hill Education, New York, United States, 904 pages, ISBN-13: 978-0-07-802410-8

[1]: 42; [2]: 42; [3]: 79; [4]: 79; [5]: 79; [6]: 79; [7]: 91; [8]: 185; [9]: 186; [10]: 201; [11]: 197; [12]: 197; [13]: 199; [14]: 197; [15]: 338-339; [16]: 339; [17]: 339; [18]: 339; [19]: 191; [20]: 264; [21]: 265; [22]: 272; [23]: 250-262; [24]: 372; [25]: 378; [26]: 136; [27]: 136; [28]: 139; [29]: 151; [30]: 162; [31]: 153; [32]: 153; [33]: 548-549; [34]: 551; [35]: 550; [36]: 10; [37]: 554; [38]: 477; [39]: 497; [40]: 509; [41]: 28; [42]: 667-668; [43]: 656; [44]: 659; [45]: 650; [46]: 679; [47]: 823; [48]: 824; [49]: 824; [50]: 824; [51]: 217; [52]: 221; [53]: 223; [54]: 224; [55]: 291; [56]: 292; [57]: 293; [58]: 294; [59]: 296; [60]: 605; [61]: 629; [62]: 607; [63]: 606; [64]: 606; [65]: 606; [66]: 606; [67]: 606; [68]: 607; [69]: 689; [70]: 695; [71]: 696; [72]: 693; [73]: 710; [74]: 692; [75]: 692; [76]: 372; [77]: 378; [78]: 376; [79]: 380; [80]: 382; [81]: 386; [82]: 386; [83]: 385-390; [84]: 392; [85]: 397; [86]: 419-420; [87]: 412; [88]: 418; [89]: 421; [90]: 732; [91]: 735; [92]: 736; [93]: 736; [94]: 740; [95]: 740; [96]: 736; [97]: 736; [98]: 783; [99]: 787; [100]: 788; [101]: 790&801 and [102]: 810

Section 3.7

From [1] to [42] based on Malhotra, D. & Bazerman, M. H. (2008) Negotiation Genius – How to overcome obstacles and achieve brilliant results at the bargaining table and beyond, Bantam Dell (Random House, Inc.), New York, United States, 343 pages, ISBN-13: 978-0-553-38411-6

[1]: 282; [2]: 27-30; [3]: 289-291; [4]: 72&74; [5]: 72; [6]: 74; [7]: 20; [8]: 37; [9]: 39; [10]: 74; [11]: 212; [12]: 53; [13]: 219; [14]: 219; [15]: 50; [16]: 65; [17]: 81; [18]: 31; [19]: 33; [20]: 64; [21]: 34; [22]: 34; [23]: 44; [24]: 42; [25]: 233; [26]: 239&249; [27]: 97; [28]: 44; [29]: 39; [30]: 96; [31]: 99; [32]: 76; [33]: 203; [34]: 201; [35]: 207; [36]: 214; [37]: 214; [38]: 297; [39]: 297; [40]: 299; [41]: 297 and [42]: 300

Section 3.8

From [1] to [85] based on Kotler, P. & Armstrong, G. (1999) Principios de Marketing, 7th Edition, Livros Tecnicos e Cientificos Editora, Rio de Janeiro, Brazil, 527 pages, ISBN-10: 85-216-1169-2

[1]: 23-25; [2]: 27-28; [3]: 35; [4]: 25-27; [5]: 31&34; [6]: 73; [7]: 80; [8]: 85; [9]: 97; [10]: 106; [11]: 129&165; [12]: 145; [13]: 148; [14]: 151; [15]: 160; [16]: 170; [17]: 177; [18]: 169; [19]: 170; [20]: 174; [21]: 190&195; [22]: 206; [23]: 191; [24]: 193; [25]: 193-195; [26]: 200; [27]: 195; [28]: 220-221; [29]: 228; [30]: 236; [31]: 243; [32]: 254; [33]: 257-258; [34]: 258; [35]: 261; [36]: 262; [37]: 262; [38]: 262; [39]: 262&264; [40]: 271; [41]: 272; [42]: 275; [43]: 280; [44]: 272; [45]: 285; [46]: 289; [47]: 287; [48]: 290; [49]: 297; [50]: 309; [51]: 310; [52]: 308; [53]: 320; [54]: 319; [55]: 323; [56]: 320; [57]: 321; [58]: 346; [59]: 349; [60]: 349; [61]: 330; [62]: 352; [63]: 352; [64]: 354; [65]: 354; [66]: 355; [67]: 356; [68]: 357; [69]: 357; [70]: 357; [71]: 357; [72]: 357; [73]: 369; [74]: 377; [75]: 398; [76]: 409; [77]: 410; [78]: 411; [79]: 423; [80]: 436; [81]: 443; [82]: 444; [83]: 457; [84]: 455 and [85]: 483

Section 3.9

From [1] to [47] based on Cook, T. A., Alston, R. & Raia, K. (2012) Mastering Import & Export Management, 2th Edition, Amacom (American Management Association), New York, United States, 675 pages, ISBN-13: 978-0-8144-2026-3

[1]: 287; [2]: 287; [3]: 39-40; [4]: 287; [5]: 287; [6]: 48; [7]: 200; [8]: 256; [9]: 76-79; [10]: 227; [11]: 41; [12]: 41; [13]: 41; [14]: 42; [15]: 42; [16]: 42; [17]: 42; [18]: 42; [19]: 43; [20]: 44; [21]: 44; [22]: 258; [23]: 255; [24]: 282-283; [25]: 282; [26]: 280; [27]: 285; [28]: 285; [29]: 149; [30]: 150; [31]: 151; [32]: 151; [33]: 151; [34]: 151; [35]: 151; [36]: 151; [37]: 102; [38]: 110; [39]: 106; [40]: 103&114; [41]: 105; [42]: 126; [43]: 111; [44]: 244; [45]: 246; [46]: 259 and [47]: 179-184

Section 3.10

From [1] to [60] based on Monczca, R. M.; Handfield, R. B.; Giunipero, L. C. & Patterson, J. L. (2016) Purchasing & Supply Chain Management, 6th Edition, Cengage Learning, Boston, United States, 858 pages, ISBN-13: 978-1-285-86968-1

[1]: 89; [2]: 377; [3]: 126; [4]: 162; [5]: 162; [6]: 108; [7]: 43; [8]: 43; [9]: 43; [10]: 43; [11]: 65; [12]: 62; [13]: 64; [14]: 64; [15]: 64; [16]: 256; [17]: 256; [18]: 256; [19]: 257; [20]: 260; [21]: 65; [22]: 196&510; [23]: 46; [24]: 219; [25]: 721; [26]: 288; [27]: 291; [28]: 292; [29]: 303; [30]: 306; [31]: 663; [32]: 665; [33]: 668; [34]: 674; [35]: 684; [36]: 381; [37]: 402; [38]: 393; [39]: 393; [40]: 547&549; [41]: 537; [42]: 553; [43]: 590; [44]: 552; [45]: 551; [46]: 553; [47]: 601; [48]: 601; [49]: 601; [50]: 605; [51]: 603; [52]: 608; [53]: 608; [54]: 608; [55]: 750; [56]: 750; [57]: 758; [58]: 769; [59]: 770 and [60]: 770

Section 3.11

From [1] to [54] based on Mathis, R. L. & Jackson, J. H. (2006) Human Resource Management, 11th Edition, South-Western (Thomson Corporation), Ohio, United States, 606 pages, ISBN-10:0-324-28958-8

[1]: 44; [2]: 48; [3]: 52; [4]: 49; [5]: 70; [6]: 69; [7]: 60; [8]: 57; [9]: 61; [10]: 60; [11]: 194; [12]: 195; [13]: 197; [14]: 201; [15]: 206; [16]: 196; [17]: 217; [18]: 213; [19]: 236; [20]: 249; [21]: 233; [22]: 233; [23]: 269; [24]: 269&285; [25]: 273; [26]: 274; [27]: 275; [28]: 296; [29]: 315; [30]: 314; [31]: 329; [32]: 333&343; [33]: 333; [34]: 350; [35]: 355; [36]: 357; [37]: 385; [38]: 386; [39]: 376; [40]: 460&474; [41]: 475; [42]: 468-469; [43]: 474; [44]: 467; [45]: 469; [46]: 480; [47]: 485; [48]: 482; [49]: 483; [50]: 485; [51]: 494; [52]: 499; [53]: 517 and [54]: 527

Section 3.12

From [1] to [60] based on Robbins, S. P. & Judge, T. A. (2015) Organizational Behavior, 16th Edition, Pearson Education Inc., New Jersey, United States, 709 pages, ISBN-13: 978-0-13-350764-5

[1]: 359; [2]: 466; [3]: 452; [4]: 113; [5]: 96; [6]: 70; [7]: 282; [8]: 122; [9]: 124; [10]: 136; [11]: 139; [12]: 153; [13]: 154; [14]: 139; [15]: 190; [16]: 347; [17]: 346; [18]: 73-77; [19]: 235; [20]: 279; [21]: 286; [22]: 289; [23]: 265; [24]: 265; [25]: 280; [26]: 288; [27]: 322; [28]: 325; [29]: 325; [30]: 325; [31]: 325; [32]: 315; [33]: 332; [34]: 344; [35]: 348; [36]: 346; [37]: 415; [38]: 417; [39]: 416; [40]: 419; [41]: 439; [42]: 434; [43]: 433; [44]: 436; [45]: 437; [46]: 477; [47]: 466; [48]: 468; [49]: 499; [50]: 503-505; [51]: 507; [52]: 512; [53]: 507; [54]: 517; [55]: 534; [56]: 535; [57]: 537; [58]: 546-548; [59]: 551 and [60]: 557

Section 3.13

From [1] to [57] based on Warren, C. S.; Reeve, J. M. & Duchac, J. E. (2016) Accounting, 26th Edition, Cengage Learning, Boston, United States, 1254 pages, ISBN-13: 978-1-285-74361-5

[1]: 3; [2]: 3; [3]: 3; [4]: 4; [5]: 4; [6]: 71; [7]: 801; [8]: 801; [9]: 117; [10]: 118; [11]: 417; [12]: 421; [13]: 228; [14]: 507; [15]: 508-510; [16]: 516-517; [17]: 517; [18]: 521; [19]: 373; [20]: 374; [21]: 376; [22]: 374; [23]: 375; [24]: 375; [25]: 376; [26]: 380; [27]: 378-380; [28]: 816; [29]: 816; [30]: 552; [31]: 559; [32]: 563; [33]: 564; [34]: 564; [35]: 684; [36]: 685; [37]: 685; [38]: 685; [39]: 700; [40]: 605; [41]: 995; [42]: 995; [43]: 998; [44]: 980; [45]: 986; [46]: 986; [47]: 1168; [48]: 1171; [49]: 1183; [50]: 1126-1128; [51]: 1082; [52]: 1124; [53]: 1132; [54]: 1037-1050; [55]: 1218; [56]: 1230 and [57]: 1232

Section 3.14

From [1] to [21] based on Bullivant, G. (2010) Credit Management, 6^a Edition, Gower Publishing Limited (Ashgate Publishing Company), Surrey, England, 735 pages, ISBN-13: 978-0-566-08842-1

[1]: 51; [2]: 63; [3]: 90; [4]: 117; [5]: 92-93; [6]: 201-202; [7]: 421; [8]: 163; [9]: 280; [10]: 188-189; [11]: 190; [12]: 354; [13]: 284; [14]: 324; [15]: 320; [16]: 273; [17]: 343; [18]: 388; [19]: 635-639; [20]: 639 and [21]: 656

Section 3.15

From [1] to [76] based on Brealey, R. A.; Myers, S. C. & Allen, F. (2008) Principios de Finanças Corporativas, 8th Edition, McGraw-Hill Interamericana, Sao Paulo, Brazil, 918 pages, ISBN-13: 978-85-7726-017-1

[1]: 374; [2]: 163; [3]: 432; [4]: 423; [5]: 463; [6]: 411-412; [7]: 362; [8]: 365; [9]: 365; [10]: 381; [11]: 365; [12]: 381; [13]: 101; [14]: 697; [15]: 693; [16]: 729; [17]: 728; [18]: 722; [19]: 722; [20]: 101; [21]: 129; [22]: 135; [23]: 640; [24]: 670; [25]: 189; [26]: 202; [27]: 203; [28]: 203&677; [29]: 55; [30]: 64; [31]: 319; [32]: 318; [33]: 319; [34]: 338; [35]: 351; [36]: 339; [37]: 339; [38]: 341; [39]: 340; [40]: 340; [41]: 340; [42]: 589; [43]: 608; [44]: 600; [45]: 603; [46]: 600; [47]: 604; [48]: 477&496; [49]: 477; [50]: 500; [51]: 505; [52]: 508; [53]: 445; [54]: 445; [55]: 445; [56]: 523; [57]: 524; [58]: 539; [59]: 523; [60]: 528; [61]: 530-534; [62]: 533; [63]: 533; [64]: 539; [65]: 618; [66]: 622; [67]: 618; [68]: 774; [69]: 774; [70]: 781; [71]: 783; [72]: 805; [73]: 809; [74]: 809; [75]: 811 and [76]: 811

Section 3.16

From [1] to [13] based on Mankiw, N. G. (1999) Introducao a Economia – Principios de Micro e Macroeconomia, Editora Campus, Rio de Janeiro, Brazil, 805 pages, ISBN-10: 85-352-0393-1

[1]: 268; [2]: 269; [3]: 270; [4]: 271; [5]: 271; [6]: 280-281; [7]: 312; [8]: 317; [9]: 330; [10]: 331; [11]: 359-360; [12]: 628 and [13]: 629

Section 3.17

From [1] to [36] based on Rejda, G. E. & McNamara, M. J. (2014) Principles of Risk Management and Insurance, 12th Edition, Pearson Education Inc., Nova Jersey, United States, 702 pages, ISBN-13: 978-0-13-299291-6

[1]: 22-23; [2]: 45; [3]: 46; [4]: 46; [5]: 47; [6]: 47; [7]: 71; [8]: 47; [9]: 55; [10]: 71; [11]: 80; [12]: 48; [13]: 106; [14]: 110; [15]: 47; [16]: 47; [17]: 48; [18]: 51; [19]: 45; [20]: 110; [21]: 109; [22]: 110; [23]: 108; [24]: 109; [25]: 201; [26]: 235; [27]: 329; [28]: 329; [29]: 356; [30]: 106; [31]: 427; [32]: 435; [33]: 462; [34]: 581; [35]: 588 and [36]: 589

Section 3.18

From [1] to [43] based on Tricker, R. (2010) ISO 9001:2008 for small businesses, 4th edition, Butterworth-Heinemann (Elsevier), Oxford, United Kingdom, 458 pages, ISBN-13: 978-1-85617-861-7

[1]: 53; [2]: 120; [3]: 68; [4]: 72; [5]: 121; [6]: 161; [7]: 181; [8]: 18-19; [9]: 14; [10]: 82-83; [11]: 97; [12]: 121; [13]: 96; [14]: 125; [15]: 93; [16]: 164; [17]: 425; [18]: 442; [19]: 147; [20]: 384; [21]: 160; [22]: 306; [23]: 300; [24]: 40; [25]: 4; [26]: 179; [27]: 174; [28]: 434; [29]: 309; [30]: 309; [31]: 443; [32]: 443; [33]: 443; [34]: 441; [35]: 348; [36]: 352; [37]: 353; [38]: 314; [39]: 311; [40]: 311; [41]: 134; [42]: 134 and [43]: 134

Section 3.19

From [1] to [46] based on Haider, S. I. (2011) Environmental Management System ISO 14001:2004 – Handbook of transition with CD-ROM, CRC Press (Taylor & Francis Group), Boca Raton, United States, 575 pages, ISBN-13: 978-1-4398-2939-4

[1]: 30; [2]: 90; [3]: 29; [4]: 171; [5]: 147; [6]: 106; [7]: 84; [8]: 106-107; [9]: 112; [10]: 111; [11]: 110; [12]: 110; [13]: 206-207; [14]: 206; [15]: 206; [16]: 154; [17]: 149; [18]: 149; [19]: 149; [20]: 260; [21]: 260; [22]: 203; [23]: 260; [24]: 260; [25]: 260; [26]: 462; [27]: 260; [28]: 218; [29]: 228; [30]: 206; [31]: 228; [32]: 228; [33]: 228; [34]: 228; [35]: 238; [36]: 238; [37]: 237; [38]: 238; [39]: 238; [40]: 174; [41]: 175; [42]: 175; [43]: 180; [44]: 180; [45]: 180&238 and [46]: 180

Section 3.20

From [1] to [9] based on United Nations (2016) Millennium Development Goals, http://www.un.org/millenniumgoals/ (accessed on May 1st, 2016)

From [10] to [33] based on Kotler, P. & Lee, N. (2005) Corporate Social Responsibility – Doing the most good for your company and your cause, John Wiley & Sons, Inc., New Jersey, United States, 307 pages, ISBN-13: 978-0-471-47611-5
[10]: 9; [11]: 10; [12]: 13; [13]: 12; [14]: 13-14; [15]: 16; [16]: 17; [17]: 17; [18]: 17; [19]: 17; [20]: 17; [21]: 17; [22]:17; [23]: 18; [24]: 18-19; [25]: 272; [26]: 91; [27]: 272; [28]: 187; [29]: 51-52; [30]: 114; [31]: 257; [32]: 268 and [33]: 274

Section 3.21

From [1] to [46] based on Geltner, D. M.; Miller, N. G.; Clayton, J. & Eichholtz, P. (2007) Commercial Real Estate Analysis & Investments, 2th Edition, Cengage Learning, Mason, United States, 848 pages, ISBN-13: 978-0-324-30548-7

[1]: 288; [2]: 269; [3]: 268; [4]: 269; [5]: 4-5; [6]: 268; [7]: 269; [8]: 63; [9]: 64; [10]: 64; [11]: 813; [12]: 822; [13]: 824; [14]: 826; [15]: 202; [16]: 236; [17]: 243; [18]: 782; [19]: 524; [20]: 324; [21]: 627-628; [22]: 628; [23]: 628; [24]: 652; [25]: 733; [26]: 733; [27]: 739; [28]: 739; [29]: 741; [30]: 742; [31]: 758; [32]: 758; [33]: 758; [34]: 759; [35]: 758; [36]: 763; [37]: 763; [38]: 768; [39]: 771; [40]: 780; [41]: 775; [42]: 795; [43]: 800; [44]: 799; [45]: 800 and [46]: 770

Section 4.1

[1] based on Blog Bring It (2014) As cinco maiores fabricantes de computadores do mundo http://blogbringit.com.br/home/as-cinco-maiores-fabricantes-de-computadores-do-mundo (accessed on May 24th, 2016 & published on December 18th, 2014)

[2] based on Lenovo (2016) Lenovo http://www.lenovo.com/br/pt/ (accessed on May 24th, 2016)

[3] based on Hewlett Packard (2016) HP http://www8.hp.com/br/pt/home.html (accessed on May 24th, 2016)

[4] based on Dell (2016) Dell http://www.dell.com/br/p/deals (accessed on May 24th, 2016)

[5]   based   on   Acer   (2016)   Acer
http://www.acer.com/ac/pt/BR/content/home   (accessed on
May 24th, 2016)

[6] based on Apple (2016) Apple http://www.apple.com/br/
(accessed on May 24th, 2016)

Section 4.2

From [1] to [13] based on Microsoft (2016) Microsoft
https://www.microsoft.com/pt-br/ (accessed on May 24th,
2016)